Introduction to Texas Politics

Introduction to Texas Politics

SIXTH EDITION

ERNEST CRAIN
San Antonio College

JAMES PERKINS
San Antonio College

THOMSON

WADSWORTH

Australia • Brazil • Canada • Mexico • Singapore
Spain • United Kingdom • United States

THOMSON
™
WADSWORTH

Introduction to Texas Politics, **Sixth Edition**
Ernest Crain and James Perkins

Executive Editor: David Tatom
Associate Assistant Editor: Rebecca Green
Editorial Assistant: Eva Dickerson
Technology Project Manager: Michelle Vardeman
Marketing Manager: Janise Fry
Marketing Assistant: Teresa Jessen
Marketing Communications Manager: Kelley McAllister
Senior Project Manager, Editorial Production: Kimberly Adams
Creative Director: Rob Hugel
Executive Art Director: Maria Epes

Print Buyer: Judy Inouye
Permissions Editor: Kiely Sisk
Production Service: International Typesetting and Composition
Photo Researcher: Linda Sykes
Copy Editor: Cheryl Smith
Cover Designer: Brian Salisbury
Cover Image: Kenny Braun
Cover Printer: Transcontinental Printing/Louiseville
Compositor: International Typesetting and Composition
Printer: Transcontinental Printing/Louiseville

Library of Congress Control Number: 2006900665

ISBN 0-495-00756-0

Thomson Higher Education
10 Davis Drive
Belmont, CA 94002-3098
USA

For more information about our products, contact us at:
Thomson Learning Academic Resource Center
1-800-423-0563
For permission to use material from this text or product, submit a request online at
http://www.thomsonrights.com.
Any additional questions about permissions can be submittted by e-mail to
thomsonrights@thomson.com.

To My Grandmother:
How big is Texas, Pa,
That people call it great?
Is it big as Heaven, Pa,
Where swings the golden gate?

'Tis not the bigness, My Son,
Of Texas that makes it great—
It was the blood of heroes
That opened Heaven's gate!
—May Myers Callaway

Brief Contents

Contents

Preface

Introduction to Texas Politics is intended as a complement to a comprehensive national government text and is to be used in an integrated course in which both national and state governments are studied. Many political issues, trends, and structures affect the entire American political system, but this text is designed to focus primarily on political and structural characteristics unique to Texas. It compares and contrasts the Texas government with the other states and the national government.

Special characteristics of Texas government have resulted from its history as part of the Old South and the Reconstruction that followed the Civil War. As a result, major themes are still woven into the fabric of Texas government: a conservative political culture, weak political parties and strong interest groups, a detailed state constitution, fragmentation of executive and judicial power at the state level, and decentralization of power in local governments.

Texas is a dynamic state. Its once land-based economy, largely dependent on the agriculture and oil industries, has been transformed by the growth of newer high-tech, biotech, tourist, financial, and service industries. Texas is becoming an international trading center as a consequence of the North American Free Trade Agreement (NAFTA) and the recent Central American Free Trade Agreement (CAFTA). Still, prosperity remains elusive. Although Texas has its share of millionaires, the stereotype of oil and cattle barons never fit the average Texan. In 2002, Texas's per capita income was $28,551 (7.7 percent below the national average), ranking it below twenty-nine other states. In 2001, 15.2 percent of Texans lived below the poverty level.

Texas has become the second most populous state and one of the most urban (more than 80 percent of Texans now live in urban areas). Migration from other states and nations has also had a dramatic impact on Texas society. Its population has become more ethnically diverse. According to the 2000 census almost 47 percent of Texans are members of ethnic minority groups, and by the next census in 2010 ethnic minorities will outnumber Anglo-Americans.

Texas's political culture remains conservative, but its political institutions have changed. Historically, conservatism was expressed by the election of old-style

Southern Democrats to virtually every office in the state. But in recent elections Republicans have taken control of both houses of the legislature and have won all statewide offices. Although Democrats have some pockets of strength in central cities, south Texas, and a few other areas, Texas has become one of the most reliably Republican states in the nation.

This new edition has been written to reflect the dynamic nature of Texas politics It includes

- Current election statistics
- Changes in the state constitution
- New economic and demographic data
- Updated legislative district maps and party control of each
- Expanded coverage of judicial selection
- Recent crime statistics
- Changes in criminal law
- New taxing and spending statistics
- Significant revision in the coverage of city government
- Helpful new websites.

1

The Texas Political Environment

INTRODUCTION

Author John Steinbeck has written, "Texas is more than a state in the union. It is a state of mind." Something about Texas has inspired generations of immigrants to come to a place that they believed was a magical land of unlimited opportunity to build a life, raise a family, and become wealthy. This image of Texas has been nurtured over the years by diverse media, including plays, dime novels, penny postcards, western pulp fiction, movies, and television. In other words, powerful myths about Texas have been created.

FIGURE 1.1   Santa Anna Being Presented to Sam Houston

The Power of Myth,[1] a popular book by Joseph Campbell and a public television series produced by Texan Bill Moyers, has helped to focus the public's attention on myths and their importance in modern society. This attention encouraged Rollo May to discuss the importance of myth in America in his book, *The Cry for Myth.* According to May, myth is important in at least three ways. First, it gives a sense of personal identity. Second, myth makes possible our sense of community. Finally, myths support our moral values.[2] The need for a powerful contemporary myth is illustrated by professional sports in Texas. Texans feel a great sense of pride and excitement over the accomplishment of the Dallas Cowboys, in spite of the fact that most of the Dallas Cowboys were not born in Texas. The players and coach are "bought" from all over the country, and may have no loyalty to Texas; only to their own jobs.[3] The most rabid fan in Dallas may have moved from Illinois only last year. Another sport, basketball, is a good example of both myth making and the impact of the global economy. The NBA champion San Antonio Spurs were powered to the 2003 and 2005 championships by such foreign players as Tim Duncan (Virgin Islands), Tony Parker (France), and Emanuel Ginobili (Argentina).[4]

Such is the power of myth to give a sense of identity and a sense of community. Let us examine the key historical stories that have influenced the major Texas myths and had a powerful impact on political values and institutions.

TEXAS MYTHS

Early Texas history laid the groundwork for later myth making. Three signal occurrences formed the basis for the creation of the Texas mystique.[5] The first incident was the Battle of the Alamo, with the titanic figures associated with it, and the creation of the Republic of Texas. Texans fought against overwhelming odds at the Alamo and lost, but were able to triumph over the Mexican army in the Battle of San Jacinto in 1836. The significance of this historic-mythical act was the "founding" of the Texas nation. Texas, like Hawaii, was once an independent nation (1836–1845) before becoming part of the United States, a fact that has generated an intense Texas nationalism that has never subsided. For example, in 1984, the state comptroller's office published a report comparing the state of Texas to nations of the world.[6]

The second myth-making situation was the long-term existence of the Texas Rangers and their immense popularity as figures of frontier justice. The Rangers are the oldest state law enforcement agency in North America, created out of the state militia organization in 1835. The Texas Rangers fought in the Mexican War of 1846 as scouts for the United States Army led by General Zachary Taylor. In the 1870s and 1880s, the Rangers provided law and order on the Texas frontier. The history of the Rangers in the twentieth century is much more controversial. The role of the Rangers was mostly to provide law enforcement support for rural sheriffs and small-town police departments faced with major crimes. However, the force became controversial among Hispanics for breaking up strikes of agricultural workers in the Rio Grande Valley.

The third mythical condition was the cattle drives following the American Civil War, which created the greatest epic expression of the generic American hero, the cowboy. The cowboy was a rugged individual who battled hostile terrain, weather, and Indians on the frontier to carve out a living—in the process, creating a whole way of life. Hollywood movies certainly played a major part in creating the mythical cowboy from the real thing. Probably no one person played this role better than John Wayne. John Wayne also figures in the creation of the Alamo myth with his construction of a copy of the Alamo in Brackettville, Texas, which was used in the filming of the movie, *The Alamo.*

It is important to state that these myths have primarily been the myths of the white Anglo population. In the tale of Texas, the contributions of Mexican Americans and African Americans have not been included in the history books. Largely because of recent scholarship and an emphasis on multiculturalism, there is now an awareness that numerous *vaqueros,* or Mexican American cowboys, and African American cowboys were just as heroic on the frontier as were Anglo cowboys. Myth, then, is a merging of fact and fiction that provides a basis for societal action. Let us relate the impact that these myths have had on political concepts in Texas.

TEXAS POLITICAL CULTURE

Political culture can be defined as the attitudes, habits, and general behavior patterns that people have in relation to their government. These attitudes reflect three major issues: (1) What is the proper role of government in society? (2) What is the proper means of participation in society or, in other words, what is a citizen's duty? (3) How are the government institutions and officeholders performing their duties?

In his book *American Federalism: A View from the States,* political scientist Daniel Elazar has developed the idea of three distinct political subcultures that have been created in the United States.[7] The first of these subcultures is Moralistic. Individuals who hold this view believe that (1) Government is necessary to promote the public good. Government should regulate society to protect the economically weak, such as children, the elderly, and the poor. (2) Each citizen has a responsibility to participate in society by being informed on issues and voting. (3) Government service is public service, and public officials should not benefit personally from holding a government office. It is the responsibility of citizens to vote out of office officials who violate this trust.

The second subculture, according to Elazar, is Individualistic. Citizens with this view believe that (1) Government should be limited only to essential functions. Individuals should be free to pursue their interests to the best of their abilities. This concept of government goes hand-in-hand with a laissez-faire economic theory. (2) Participation by the average citizen is discouraged. Generally, the wealthy and educated elite are the individuals who should vote because they understand the proper relationship between the economy and the government. (3) The evaluation of the government should be left to experts. Government service is like operating a large business. Officeholders are paid well because of their expertise and hard work.

The final subculture developed by Elazar is Traditionalistic. Those with this viewpoint hold that (1) Government is expected to preserve the social order and the relative position of the various social classes. (2) Participation by the lower classes is usually discouraged by law. (3) Government service is dominated by the elite social class. This subculture is very similar to the Individualistic, with the key difference being the emphasis on social class.

The overall political culture of Texas, based on these models, is generally a mixture of Individualistic and Traditionalistic. The Moralistic culture seems to prevail only in the Panhandle region. Elazar concludes that the Traditionalistic subculture is slightly more important in Texas, which means that the dominant socioeconomic class, Anglo-Texans, has largely dominated Texas government. The participation of average citizens was actively discouraged through laws such as the poll tax, annual voter registration, and the white primary. (These topics will be fully developed in Chapter 3.) The activities of government are limited to maintaining law and order so that individuals, both rich and poor, have the maximum amount of freedom to pursue their individual interests. The wealthy generally have an advantage over the poor in pursuing their interests.

To understand how these myths and cultural values have been translated into government structures and processes today, it is helpful to examine how the geographic characteristics, the pattern of immigration, and historical events have shaped Texas.

The Land

Texas is a vast landscape that stretches from the central time zone in East Texas to the mountain time zone in West Texas. It is almost 800 miles from Texarkana, on the Arkansas border, to El Paso, on the Rio Grande. Texas is the second largest state in the union, with 267,339 square miles of territory. This vast size is one of the factors that helped to boost the myth of Texas as a virtual nation unto itself. Under this landscape is tremendous mineral wealth, which would become another important factor in the development of Texas.

Most of Texas's earliest settlers were attracted by the diversity and richness of its land. The East Texas marsh and forestland gradually gives way to the fertile black prairie land of Central Texas and the coastal plain farther southward. Moving westward across the Balcones escarpment, one begins to encounter the Hill Country area northwest of San Antonio. The rolling plains stretch from Fort Worth to points beyond Wichita Falls and Abilene, while, farther west, the rolling hills fade into the plains of the Lubbock and Pan handle area. Across the Pecos, near-desert conditions surround the spectacular Davis and Guadalupe mountains, some of which are as high as the Rockies.

Early settlers brought cotton farming from the Old South to Central Texas and the "piney woods" of East Texas, but other types of farming and ranching are now more significant in these regions. Twentieth-century irrigation methods have made it possible for the declining Ogallala aquifer to continue to support cotton and grain production in the plains around Lubbock and Amarillo to an extent unprecedented in the state's history. Sheep and goats thrive in the Hill Country area. Miscellaneous farms dot the landscape between East Texas and the desert lands that lie beyond the Pecos; spread between the farms are the pasturelands that make the cattle, cowboy boots, and Stetson hats all too synonymous with Texas. To complete the picture, great mineral wealth, such as oil, was found first in East Texas and later in the West as well.

The People and Their Backgrounds

For several centuries, Texas's varied lands attracted successive waves of migration both from the United States and from other countries.

Native Americans The first Paleo-American peoples began to settle in Texas around 10,000 B.C., attracted by the abundance of game and fresh water. No one particular tribe or nation dominated in Texas, as the sprawling state became the melting pot of four distinct cultural types: the Western Gulf Culture, the Plains, Southeast Culture, and Southwest Culture.[8] The competition for resources reduced the numbers of tribes over the centuries. In the 1700s, Lipan Apaches and the Comanche tribes became preeminent, and fought fierce battles with settlers in West Texas until the late 1870s. Today there are only three tribes living on reservations and recognized by the U.S. government: The Alabama-Coushatta tribe, living in East Texas; the Tigua tribe in West Texas near El Paso; and the Kickapoo, living on the border near Eagle Pass. Native Americans in Texas today make up less than 0.5 percent of the total population.

Although Native American culture did not influence Texas political and social institutions, it did leave a lasting legacy. The Spanish called the Caddo Indians they encountered "Tejas," meaning "friends." It became the name of the whole region, Texas!

Mexican Americans   One of the first Spanish explorers to see Texas was Alvar Nuñez Cabeza de Vaca. Shipwrecked on the Texas Gulf Coast in 1528, Cabeza de Vaca spent six years living among different Native American tribes in South Texas. When Cabeza de Vaca finally returned to an outpost in northern Mexico, his tales of great riches and golden cities spurred additional Spanish exploration of Texas. These tales probably started the first myths about Texas.

In 1716, the first Spanish missions were established in East Texas to lay claim to this territory, and to prepare the land for colonization. This effort had a major impact on Texas, as cattle and horses from the missions strayed into the wild and reproduced. As a result of this, Native American tribes became more mobile and able to challenge frontier settlers, and, later, tens of thousands of wild cattle provided the basis for the cattle industry in Texas.

In 1821, Mexico won independence from Spain, and Texas became an obscure province of Mexico. In the 1830s Anglo immigrants, primarily from the southern United States, poured into Texas and tensions began to increase between Mexican settlers and the newcomers. After the epic battles of the Alamo and San Jacinto, Texas became independent from Mexico in 1836, and Anglos pushed the earlier settlers southward, thereby gaining control of much of their land. The Mexican War of 1846 produced a climate in Texas of systematic discrimination against Mexican Americans. In the late 1800s, the Mexican American population in Texas declined to about 4 percent of the total.

Early twentieth-century political upheavals in Mexico brought a new wave of immigrants, who settled in South and Southwest Texas, around the few remaining pockets of Hispanic culture. Anglo entrepreneurs, farmers, and ranchers often welcomed the Mexicans as a cheap source of labor, but not as equal participants in Texas's prosperity. In spite of persistent political, social, and economic inequality, legal and illegal immigration has continued to accelerate, largely because of Mexico's poverty.

The Mexican American population in Texas tends to be concentrated in South Texas along the border with Mexico and in the major urban centers of Houston and Austin. Hispanics make up the majority of the population in the third and fourth largest cities in Texas, San Antonio and El Paso. The 2000 census revealed that Mexican Americans are 25.5 percent of the state population, and the trend is clear that this percentage will continue to increase in the twenty-first century. Mexican Americans have made important strides in reducing political, social, and economic inequality by increasing their voting, and by electing Mexican Americans to the state legislature and to statewide office.

African Americans   African Americans did not begin to come to Texas in large numbers until the Republic of Texas was created in 1836. Neither the Spanish nor Mexican governments allowed slavery. The majority of Anglo-American immigrants coming to Texas, particularly from the Lower South (Louisiana, Mississippi, Alabama, and Georgia), brought slaves with them. Although African Americans were freed after the Civil War, economic and state political discrimination kept African Americans from exercising their legal rights. African Americans tended to remain in East Texas and migrated to population centers closest to the area, Houston and Dallas. In 1990, the African American population in Texas was slightly less than 12 percent. With the passage of the national Voting Rights Act in 1965, and various amendments since, African Americans have been able to elect members to the Texas legislature to represent them in their struggle for equality.

Anglo Americans   When, in the early nineteenth century, Mexico issued land grants to *empressarios* such as Stephen F. Austin, Anglos began to establish their roots in Texas. They first settled in the rich lands of Central Texas, between the Colorado and Trinity Rivers, but soon migrated to every other region of the state, establishing themselves as the predominant ethnic group. Immigrants directly from Europe—Germans, Czechs, Poles, and Norwegians—began to establish a few settlements in Central Texas in the late 1840s; the largest group was the Germans, who populated the Hill Country area. A significant number of residents in the Panhandle and North Texas regions trace their ancestry to non-southern areas such as the United States's Midwest region. The state's pleasant climate and favorable economic situation have continued to attract many people from around the country.

The Anglo population has generally used political institutions to control government power, even where there were overwhelming majorities of non-Anglos in South Texas, East Texas, and major urban areas. In 1990, the Anglo population in Texas was 60 percent of the total population, but population trends indicate that by 2026, Anglos will make up only 47 percent of the population. This will mean that no one racial or ethnic group will constitute a majority.

Asian Americans   The fastest growing and newest wave of immigrants to Texas are from Asia. Eighty percent of these immigrants are refugees from Southeast Asia, especially Vietnam, Cambodia, and Laos.[9] The United States's involvement in the Vietnam War is largely responsible for this. Refugees, who are different from other legal immigrants, have been persecuted in their native land or have a well-founded fear of persecution. Asian Americans were almost 2 percent of the state's population in 1990. The trend is for this group to continue to grow in numbers in the next decade.

REGIONAL DEVELOPMENT

The cumulative effect of the migration patterns into Texas, together with the various economic and geographic realities of the state have resulted in the distinctive cultural areas shown in Figure 1.2. Again, although generalizations must be used, the characteristics of individual areas are evident and can help to explain the diverse politics of the state.

East Texas

Basically, East Texas society is rural and biracial. In spite of the changes brought about by civil rights legislation, "black towns" exist side by side with "white towns," and there are still many essentially segregated social and economic institutions such as churches, chambers of commerce, and shopping areas.

FIGURE 1.2 Modern Texas Regions

East Texas is very much a social and cultural extension of the Old South. Old families whose wealth is founded in land, banking, and retail merchandising often dominate counties or towns. Here cotton is no longer "king," having been supplanted by the cultivation of beef cattle, poultry, and timber. Because of a general lack of economic opportunity, the migration of young East Texans to the rapidly developing urban areas continues. This decline in population, plus the rapid growth of other parts of the state, means that East Texas no longer plays the dominant cultural and political role it once did.

The Gulf Coast

Before 1900, Texas was essentially an *economic colony:* that is, it sold raw materials to the industrialized North and bought northern-manufactured products. In 1901, however, an oil well called Spindletop was drilled near the town of Beaumont, and Texas was never the same again. Since that time, most of the Gulf Coast has experienced an almost continuous boom. In addition to being an industrial center, it is one of the most important shipping centers in the nation. Spindletop was backed by Eastern money, and its success stimulated increased Eastern investment in the state—a significant amount of industry is still owned by outside investors. Local wealth, too, was generated, and was then largely reinvested in Texas to promote the long-range industrial development of the state. At the same time, considerable income continues to come from the sale of raw materials.

The influx of job seekers from East Texas and other agricultural areas of the state has given the urban Gulf Coast some of the flavor of rural Texas. In addition, there are a substantial number of well-educated young executives who have come from the northern and western United States. Primarily, the social and economic elite consists of the newly rich (from oil, insurance, and banking investments) and the office and plant managers who are employed by national businesses. There are many large ranches and plantations, often absentee-owned by wealthy oil or business executives who prefer to live in the large cities. The area is cosmopolitan, has a modern outlook, and is less bound by tradition than most other parts of the state.

North Texas

North Texas is a buffer between East and West Texas, containing many of the characteristics of both. Cotton, small grains, and livestock are produced in substantial quantities on its black land prairies.

In the 1880s, railroads came into Texas from the northern United States. Because of its geographic location, Dallas became a rail center and grew rapidly in population and commercial activity, stimulated by both people and capital from the North. This new rail center was developed at Houston's expense, and as the latter city lost much of its initial commercial lead, the coast temporarily lost popularity as an outlet for Texas raw materials. Fort Worth then became a regional capital and looked primarily to West Texas for growth and trade. The Swift and Armour meatpacking companies moved into Fort Worth in 1901, the first national firms to establish plants close to Texas's natural resources. More businesses followed, and Texas began its slow transformation from an economic colony to an industrial leader.

Today, North Texas is a center for defense-related industries, as well as for the production of electronic equipment, computer products, plastics, food products, and aircraft. Dallas and Fort Worth exhibit the same cosmopolitan characteristics evident on the Gulf Coast. Dallas remains a banking and commercial center of national importance, and Fort Worth, the commercial center for the entire West Texas area, is still "the city where the West begins."

West Texas

West Texas is the largest of the state's modern cultural areas and is usually thought of as "cattle country." Because the scarcity of water and grass required large acreage for economically viable cattle operations, giant ranches became common after the Apaches were defeated in the 1880s. Modern West Texas's economy is supported by ranching and petroleum production, and by vegetable and cotton production, made possible by extensive irrigation. Primarily sheep and goats, as well as cattle, are raised in the southern part of this region. Northern West Texas's main agricultural activity is irrigated farming.

Oil is produced in almost all West Texas counties, and in major quantities in many. Several of its cities, such as Snyder, Midland, and Odessa, owe their existence almost entirely to oil and its related industries.

There are few African Americans living in West Texas; recently, Mexican Americans have begun to migrate into the region in significant numbers, settling mainly in the intensively farmed areas. Because immigrants from the southern United States primarily settled the area, West Texas is fundamentalist in its religious outlook and conservative-Democrat and Republican in its political viewpoint.

The Panhandle

The building of railroads from Kansas City through the Texas Panhandle brought Midwest farmers into this region, and it was the immigrants from Kansas who introduced wheat production to the area. Because the commercial and cultural focus of the region was, and still is, toward Kansas City rather than the developed areas in Texas, the Panhandle continues to be basically Midwestern in both character and institutions. The political conservatism of the area is more Republican than Southern Democrat, and its churches are more moralistic in political culture, philosophy, and practice.

Southwest Texas

Anglo-American ranchers and Hispanic *vaqueros,* or herdsmen, share this area. Southwest Texas has always been sparsely populated and is definitely ranch country. Its economy is based on goats, sheep, cattle, and tourism. El Paso, the major city, looks economically and culturally to New Mexico and Mexico, rather than to the rest of Texas.

South Texas

Both "The Valley" (of the Rio Grande River) and the "Winter Garden" (around Crystal City) are in South Texas. Immigrants from the North mainly settled the Valley in the 1920s. This coincided with similar growth patterns in southern Florida, California, and Arizona. The farming of citrus fruits (the climate here favors agriculture), tourism, and developing retirement communities dominate the economy's growth.

The area's economic growth has created new job opportunities for field laborers, who are needed to work with the citrus and vegetable crops. As a consequence, immigration from Mexico has increased. As with African Americans in East Texas, South Texas has dual social and economic systems, and its "Mexican" towns exist side by side with "Anglo" towns. Roman Catholic Mexican Americans often retain strong links with Mexico through extended families and friends, and by continuing to speak Spanish and read Spanish-language newspapers.

The German Hill Country

The German Hill Country is still a distinct and homogeneous cultural region. Though its inhabitants have become "Americanized," they still cling to many of their cultural traditions. Primarily a farming and ranching area, this region is a stronghold of Texas Republicanism.

Central Texas

Roughly triangular in shape and bordered by the trade routes between Houston, Dallas-Fort Worth, and San Antonio, Central Texas is often called the core area of Texas. Here exist cultural traits from all the areas of Texas, although no single one dominates enough to stamp its distinctiveness on the entire region. A microcosm of Texas culture, it is diversified in terms of agriculture (cotton, grain, sheep, goats, cattle), industry, and population, which all combine into a mixture similar to that of the commercial activities found in all the other cultural areas of the state.

URBAN DEVELOPMENT

Population Movement

Urbanization   In the 1850 U.S. census, the first after Texas became a state, only 4 percent of the population was classified as urban. The definition of "urban" at that time was any place with a population of more than 1,000 inhabitants. The overwhelming majority of Texas's population lived in small towns and on farms in the eastern half of the state. The economy was largely agricultural, and people lived where the jobs were.

After the Civil War, the industrial revolution came to the northeastern part of the United States. Manufacturing brought jobs to the urban areas, and millions of Americans moved from the small towns and farms to the new industrial cities. In New York and in other industrialized states, by the 1900 census, a majority of the population lived in urban areas. In Texas, it would take World War II (1941–1945) and the vast mobilization of workers, military bases, and industry to bring the population to urban areas.

The 1950 census was the first one in which a majority of Texas's population was classified as urban, with 63 percent so designated. Since 1950, Texas has been among the top states in the United States in terms of urbanization. Since the 1960 U.S. census, the state of Texas has reached the point where 80 percent of the population lives in urban areas. Three of the nation's most populous cities are in Texas: Houston, Dallas, and San Antonio.

The striking transformation of the Texas population is not fully revealed without a careful examination of what the "80 percent urban" population means. The real story is not what percentage of people lives in urban areas; rather, it is what percentage of the population lives in metropolitan areas. The urban population has been increasing since 1940, but it has especially grown in the state's largest cities. The U.S. Census Bureau designates these cities as Metropolitan Statistical Areas (MSAs) (see Figure 1.3).

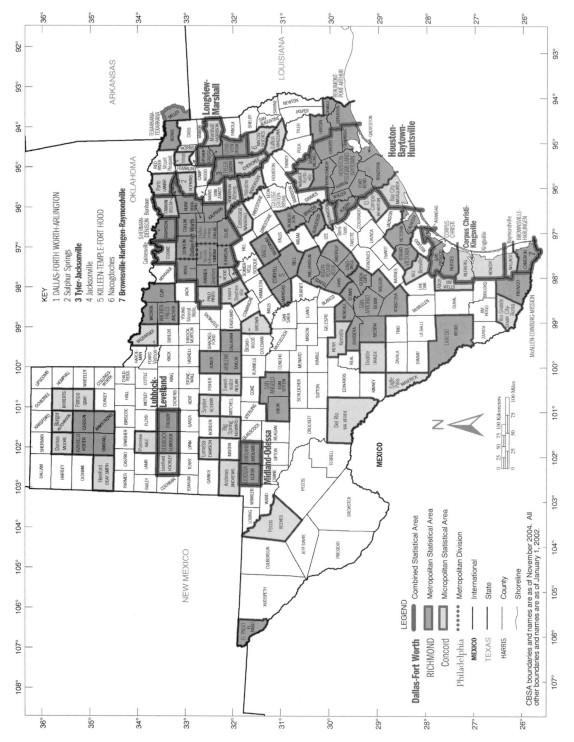

FIGURE 1.3 Texas Metro-Area Populations—1999 Estimate

SOURCE: U.S. Department of Commerce, Economics and Statistics Administration, Bureau of the Census.

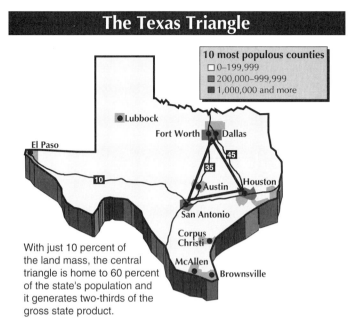

The Texas Triangle

10 most populous counties
☐ 0–199,999
▨ 200,000–999,999
■ 1,000,000 and more

Lubbock

Fort Worth • Dallas
El Paso
45
35
10
Austin • Houston
San Antonio
Corpus
Christi •
McAllen   Brownsville

With just 10 percent of the land mass, the central triangle is home to 60 percent of the state's population and it generates two-thirds of the gross state product.

FIGURE 1.4 The Texas Triangle
SOURCE: John Sharp, Texas Comptroller of Public Accounts, *Fiscal Notes* (Jan. 1994).

Suburbanization Beginning in the 1960s, a second major movement of population in the United States occurred. People began to move from central city areas to the suburbs. The Census Bureau developed new concepts to accommodate these population changes. First, the definition of an urban area was changed to an area with a population of 2,500 or more.

To reveal the extent of suburban growth, the Census Bureau developed the concepts of Primary Metropolitan Statistical Areas (PMSAs) and Consolidated Metropolitan Statistical Areas (CMSAs). In 1990, Texas had 28 MSAs, more than any other state, representing 53 counties and 81.6 percent of the state's population. In 2004, Combined Statistical Area (CBSA) was added to reflect suburban sprawl (see Figure 1.3). Not only has Texas become one of the most urbanized states, but its population is concentrated in a relatively small triangle with Dallas, Houston, and San Antonio as the points on the triangle. This area contains 60 percent of the state's population (see Figure 1.4).

Population Growth

Since the 1940 census, Texas has been among the fastest growing states in the nation. Texas's 1990 population increased 18.3 percent over 1980, to nearly 17 million people. This total made Texas the third most populous state in the nation, behind only California and New York. In the 2000 census, Texas's population was 20,852,000. This confirmed what had been suspected since 1994, that Texas had become the second most populous state in the nation. This achievement caused some Texans to celebrate the myth of Texas as among the biggest and best, but it also had very important political implications. Texas gained two new U.S. Representative seats during reapportionment. Texas now has 32 representatives in Congress, second only to California. This increase in congressional districts will also increase Texas's vote in the Electoral College to elect the president. Each state has a vote in the Electoral College equal to its number of representatives plus two (number of senators). Texas will acquire more influence in national politics. Finally, federal aid to states is typically disbursed according to a state's population. Texas thus received more federal dollars, which in 2005 accounted for 35.7 percent of the state's budget.

ECONOMIC DEVELOPMENT

Hand in hand with changes in population have come economic changes. A noted Texas historian offers the analogy of Texans as the heirs of a rich person who have wasted three inheritances. The three inheritances that the state of Texas has had are (1) cotton, (2) cattle, and (3) oil.[10] One of the first things to attract Southern immigrants to Texas was the rich black soil of East Central Texas. This soil was ideal for cotton and corn, the two most important crops in the middle 1800s, and offered the beginnings of the agricultural industry, which is still an important part of the Texas economy today. Texas ranks third among the fifty states in government payments to farmers, and first in net farm income in 2001.[11]

Cattle wealth was the legacy of the Spaniards, who introduced cattle to North America. The environment was well suited for the farming of these animals. As cattle were lost or strayed from mission settlements, they reproduced in the wild. It was estimated in the 1820s that there were tens of thousands of wild cattle in Texas from the Red River to the Rio Grande. The cattle industry grew to become one of the key elements of the Texas economy. Texas ranked first out of the fifty states, with 14.8 million cattle.

Although the first oil refinery began production of a thousand barrels of oil in Corsicana in 1898, most people put the birth of the oil industry in Texas at the Spindletop oil strike near Beaumont in East Texas, which produced 3.2 million barrels of oil in 1901, its first year. In 1928, Texas became the leading crude oil producer in the United States.[12] The demands of World War II helped to transform the oil boom into a long-term source of prosperity and made coastal Texas, particularly Houston, the petroleum center of the world.

The Texas economy in the 1960s and 1970s experienced strong, steady growth based on oil prices, the last "inheritance," on national defense spending in Texas, and on the general health of the U.S. economy. Texas was also benefiting from the movement of people from the northeastern states (the Frost Belt) to Texas and other southwestern states (the Sun Belt). In his book *Power Shift,* Kirkpatrick Sale discusses the six economic pillars on which Sun Belt states based their economic growth: agribusiness, defense industries, high-tech industries, oil, real estate, and tourism.[13]

In the early 1980s, the Texas economy peaked in oil production and real estate values. In 1981, the highest recorded level of operating oil rigs occurred, at 1,316. In 1983, Texas built 11 percent of the nation's homes and 25 percent of the nation's apartments.[14] Then, in 1986, the world oil market collapsed, and the price of West Texas intermediate crude oil fell from a high of $35 a barrel to less than $10 a barrel.

The real estate markets in oil-dependent areas collapsed, which in turn caused a number of banks and savings and loan institutions to fail. For the year 1987, more than 8,300 Texas businesses failed. Texas led the nation in commercial bank failures, with 132 in 1989. The number of active oil rigs fell to its lowest level, 266.

During the 1990s, Texas began to rebuild its economy. Agribusiness became one of the anchors of the economy, but the industry was plagued by bad weather as droughts affected South and West Texas. Other anchors were tourism and high-tech industries, as Texas tried to develop a more diversified economy. One of the real economic success stories has been in-state tourism due to the popularity of professional major league sports. The comptroller of public accounts estimates that this industry generates roughly $860 million a year for the Texas economy.[15]

High-tech industries are the vast array of businesses that all rely upon the same essential element: the silicon chip. Texas has had some success in attracting these industries, especially to the Austin area. But the prospects for future growth are troubled by two major problems. The first is the reduction of national defense spending by the U.S. government. The base reduction act has produced a decrease in defense spending, an area of government spending closely tied to high-tech industries. The second and greater problem that Texas faces is its educational system. One of the important requirements for high-tech industries is a well-trained and educated workforce. At the present time, Texas has difficulty competing with the school systems in other states that wish to attract high-tech industries. In 2000, Texas ranked thirty-first among the fifty states in per capita spending for all areas of education.[16] The average salary of a classroom teacher in 2002 placed Texas at twenty-ninth among the fifty states. This level of spending on education has a major impact on income in the state.

Income

At the heart of the myth of Texas as a special place is the idea that, with individual freedom and lack of government regulation, people can work hard and become rich. One only has to look at the example of H. Ross Perot. He started with $5,000 of borrowed money in 1961, and today he is a billionaire. However, hard work does not pay off in the same way for everyone. There is another side of reality to this myth. Minority groups in Texas, in general, have not had the same success at working hard and becoming rich. Social, economic, and political discrimination have kept many Texas citizens at poverty-level incomes or below.

In 2000, Texas ranked twenty-third out of the fifty states in personal income. Per capita figures tend to mask the reality of a few very rich and many more very poor. In Texas, 15.2 percent of the population lives at or below poverty level. In 2001, only five states (mostly in the deep South) had a greater percentage of poverty-level incomes than Texas. In another measure of the unequal distribution of wealth and income in Texas, the median household income ranked thirtieth in 2001. The key to understanding how great opportunity and great wealth can exist side by side with great poverty is in examining public education in Texas.

Education

Although Mirebeau B. Lamar, third president of the Republic of Texas, advocated a large land endowment for public education (in 1836), the growth of the education system has been erratic. The endowment has grown into the Permanent School Fund (PSF), which provides some of the revenue for K-12th grade, and the Permanent University Fund (PUF), which provides revenue for the University of Texas and Texas A&M. Due to this dedicated funding source as well as generous funding from the legislature, UT and A&M have been able to compete successfully with universities all over the world, but the rest of Texas education has not been so lucky.

When Texas is compared with educational spending in the other forty-nine states, the mediocrity of its educational system stands out. Texas ranks thirty-fourth in expenditures per pupil in elementary and secondary schools in 2000. It ranks thirty-second in average salary for public school teachers. The statistics related to the education level of the entire population reveals an even worse picture. Texas ranks thirty-sixth in the percentage of population graduated from high school in 2002, and forty-seventh among the fifty states in average Scholastic Achievement Test (SAT) scores.

What these figures tend to reveal is the influence of the Individualistic, Traditionalistic political culture on public-policy decisions in Texas. Texans generally dislike extensive public services and the taxes that are necessary to support them. In fact, an anti-intellectual feeling tends to exist in the state. Texans see education in "practical" terms, so they are interested in vocational-technical programs and the basics: reading, writing, and arithmetic. The ability to make money is often the "practical" standard of success. In addition to an anti-intellectual feeling in Texas, the state has never provided equal educational opportunity for all of its students.

First, the 1876 (current) constitution required racial segregation of its public schools. Like African Americans, Mexican Americans were also excluded, until the U.S. Supreme Court case of *Brown v. Board of Education* overturned segregation in public education in 1954.

Second, the state has never provided equal funding for public education. By examining the modern history of public education in Texas, the basic funding situation can be explained. In 1949, with the passage of the Gilmer-Aiken Act, Texas established a guarantee of at least a minimum education for all students and established the Texas Education Agency (TEA) to carry out these policies. The funding of public education was a combination of state and local independent school district (ISD) spending, with local spending based on the property wealth of each ISD. Property-rich schools were able to provide public education spending way above the state minimum, but property-poor schools could barely afford to provide the state minimum. Property-poor school districts almost always enrolled a large portion of minority students. This system of funding led to a lawsuit filed by the parents of students in a poor school district. The case, *Rodriguez v. San Antonio ISD,* was brought before the U.S. Supreme Court in 1973. The case focused a spotlight on Texas schools, but in the end the Supreme Court ruled that there was no guarantee of equal public education under the U.S. Constitution.

Over the next few years, the state legislature attempted to reform the funding for public education, but little was done until H. Ross Perot got behind efforts for a major reform plan. In 1984, the legislature passed House Bill 72, a far-reaching reform that still left the property wealth of independent school districts as a key component of funding.

Another lawsuit was filed by poor school districts, and in the case of *Edgewood I.S.D. v. Kirby* in 1989, the Texas Supreme Court ruled that the Texas school financing system violated the state constitution, and gave the Texas legislature less than one year to correct it. The Texas legislature passed a law that created county education districts (CEDs), which would pool the property wealth of rich and poor districts. However, the Texas Supreme Court in January 1992 found this new funding law to be unconstitutional.

Finally, in May 1993, the legislature passed Senate Bill 7, which directed property-rich schools to share their wealth with poor districts. This is popularly known as a Robin Hood plan—take from the rich and give to the poor. Rather than increasing public funding to bring the poor schools up to the level of richer schools, the legislature decided to bring the property-wealthy school funding down, and bring poor school funding up, to arrive at equality somewhere at a middle range.

One important funding issue remains to be resolved. School facilities remain the responsibility of local independent school districts. Usually the poor districts cannot afford new, modern facilities. The equalization of school facilities was not considered under any of the lawsuits.

The impact of funding on the current situation in public education in Texas can be demonstrated by looking at the hundred students who could represent the class of 1994, which attended kindergarten in 1981. Five of those students dropped out by the eighth grade. Twenty-three dropped out before high school. Thirty-six graduated from high school and entered the workforce, probably in a minimum wage job. Thirty-six went on to higher education. Of the thirty-six in higher education, eighteen will enter the work force with less than a bachelor's degree and will have better, but still somewhat limited, occupational choices than most of their classmates, and eighteen will enter the work force with at least a bachelor's degree.[17]

The kindergarten class of 1994 will not graduate from high school until the year 2007 and from college until 2011. The future of education in Texas is now. Providing equal educational funding for all students in Texas at a competitive level with other states is an urgent priority for today. The state must increase the number of students who graduate, both from high school and from college and universities. As the twenty-first century progresses, let us examine the forecasts of experts about the economy and demographics of Texas in the future.

TEXAS CULTURE AND POLITICS
IN THE TWENTY-FIRST CENTURY

Economics

Since New Year's Day 1994, Texas has been part of the world's largest trading bloc, linking the economies of the United States, Canada, and Mexico. The North American Free Trade Agreement (NAFTA) aims to phase out tariffs and other economic barriers among these three nations. This agreement has increased export opportunities for small and medium-sized businesses, but at the same time increased foreign product competition.[18] In 2005, Congress passed the Central American Free Trade Agreement (CAFTA) to continue the Bush administration focus on a free trade economy.

Economic experts predict that the Texas economy will continue to diversify over the next thirty-five years. Jobs in service industries, both tourism and retail trade, and in import-export businesses will greatly expand. Today, almost one-quarter of all statewide jobs are in services. By the year 2026, this figure will rise to over 30 percent.[19] The outlook for new jobs in Texas is bright, but many of these new jobs, especially in trade and services, will be in low-paying occupations, limiting the growth of wages and income. Also, the need to remain competitive in a global economy will further restrict wage growth in Texas. Energy-related industries will continue to decline in importance and employment. Defense spending of the United States will continue to decline also, with the possible closing of military bases in Texas in the future. The latest Defense Base Closure and Realignment Commission (BRAC) Report was released in September 2005 as this edition was being written.

The long-term economic news for Texas is mixed. Overall, the Texas economy should continue to expand at a moderate rate, slightly outpacing the U.S. economy. This should provide a positive reason for the Texas myth to continue to attract new immigrants. However, this growth will be at a level below the boom periods of the 1960s and 1970s, and real wage and income growth will be weak.[20] This will, of course, have the greatest impact on those workers with the least amount of education.

The terrorist attacks on New York and Washington on September 11, 2001, lead to an economic downturn, which impacted most state economies. The Texas economy was also hit by a lack of state government revenue because of tax cuts, and the lack of tax sources, such as an income tax. These and other factors produced a massive deficit for the 2003 and 2004 budget years.

The continuing war in Iraq and the rapid growth of the Chinese economy have combined to drive up the price of gasoline. This trend in gasoline prices is a real threat to continued economic growth in Texas, as in the rest of the country. [21]

Cultural Diversity

The Texas comptroller's report, *The Changing Face of Texas,* gives us a forecast of the Texas population in the twenty-first century. There are four major themes presented in the report. The first is that the Texas population will continue to grow, although at a slower rate than it has historically. It will reach over 22 million people in 2026. Second, the population will continue to age, led by the large baby boom wave, with almost 4 million Texans who are 65 years and older in 2026. Third, minorities, especially Mexican Americans, will both grow and gain in their share of the population. By 2026, Mexican Americans will constitute more than 38 percent of the population of Texas. There will be no majority racial or ethnic group, with Anglos representing less than 47 percent of the state's population.

Finally, 94 percent of the population growth in Texas in the future will be in the Metropolitan Statistical Areas (MSAs). The population will be more concentrated in metropolitan areas, with population density increasing from 65 people per square mile to 85 people per square mile in 2026.

As the population becomes more diverse in terms of race and ethnicity, age, and geographic location, this diversity will alter the myths, the political culture, and the governmental institutions and political processes in Texas.

CONCLUSION

Texas, it seems, has always been a place that holds a mysterious attraction for immigrants, from Ice Age Paleo-American peoples to southerners of the 1830s, who chalked "gone to Texas" on the doors of their houses; from Spaniards in the 1700s, seeking new territory, to Asians in the 1990s, who came from refugee camps in Southeast Asia, with the word that Houston is the "golden mountain" and the place to seek your fortune.[22] The myth of Texas as a special place has endured.

Immigrants of all kinds have built and lost personal fortunes on the abundance of the land, in crops, cattle, and oil. But the myth has had a sinister side for African American and Mexican American citizens, who have been the victims of discrimination and a public education system with unequal funding.

The future looks hopeful, but at the same time full of challenges. In the twenty-first century, no one ethnic or racial group will command a majority of the population. This will mean that the myths and political culture of the past will change and evolve. The opportunity of individual freedom and unlimited upward mobility must be extended to all citizens of Texas. The education system must be improved to provide the tools necessary for competition in the global economy in the future. NAFTA and CAFTA, perhaps, provide Texas with a golden opportunity for a fourth inheritance. The issues of terrorism and the rising price of gasoline threaten the growth of the global economy, and remain to be resolved.

To translate these goals and opportunities into concrete action requires the creation of governmental institutions and processes. in the next chapter, we look at the Texas Constitution, which provides the blueprint for action.

KEY TERMS

Central American Free
   Trade Agreement
   (CAFTA)

Edgewood v. Kirby

Individualistic

Moralistic

myth

North American Free
   Trade Agreement
   (NAFTA)

political culture

suburbanization

Traditionalistic

urbanization

Logging On: Welcome to the Internet

Welcome to cyberpolitics in Texas. The rapid development of the Web part of the Internet has created unprecedented opportunity for research, communication, and participation in Texas politics. Today, students can easily communicate with authors of their textbooks, governmental leaders, and fellow students all across Texas. To assist in this twenty-first century education, ITP has developed a Texas Government at the address: **http://www.wadsworth.com/polisci.**

Community colleges and universities in Texas are connected to the Internet. Ask your instructor how you can access the Internet at your institution. The Web offers you the opportunity to greatly expand your knowledge and understanding of government and politics in Texas. Each chapter will provide you with the URL address of sites that will enrich your understanding of the text materials. In addition to mastering knowledge of Texas government, you will also be developing skills in the education and communication technology of the future.

To begin to research the myths and political culture of Texas, we suggest the home page of the monthly magazine that presents Texas to us and to the rest of the country, *Texas Monthly.* For your first visit

to the site, you must register with your E-mail address and password. A number of free newsletters are available upon request. Our favorite feature is still the analysis of each legislative session by Paul Burka and Patricia Kilday Hart. Scroll all the way down to the miscellany section to find the Legislative Follies of 2003. *Texas Monthly* is found at **http://www.texasmonthly.com/.**

The excavation of French explorer Robert La Salle's ship *La Belle* off the coast of Texas has revealed new insights into the early European exploration of Texas. The Texas Historical Commission Website has information about projects such as the excavation of the La Belle and Texas Historical Courthouses. The story, culture, and environment of Texas is examined at a Website called "Lone Star Junction." This site offers a free 3-D Texas screensaver. Check out the many features at **http://www.lsjunction.com.**

The Institute of Texas Cultures of the University of Texas at San Antonio offers many insights into Texas history and culture. Take a mini-tour of the exhibit floor at **http://www.texancultures.utsa.edu/new/info/tour.htm.**

ENDNOTES

1. Joseph Campbell, *The Power of Myth* (New York: Doubleday), 1988.

2. Rollo May, *The Cry for Myth* (New York: W. W. Norton), 1991, pp. 30–31.

3. May's example of the San Francisco 49ers per tem website was adapted to Texas.

4. May's example applied to professional basketball.

5. Archie P. McDonald (Ed.), *The Texas Experience* (College Station: Texas A&M Press), 1986, p. 177.

6. Texas Comptroller of Public Accounts, *Fiscal Notes* (December 1984), p. 9.

7. Daniel Elazar, *American Federalism: A View from the States* (New York: Thomas Y. Crowell), 1966.

8. W. W. Newcomb, Jr., *The Indians of Texas* (Austin: Univ. of Texas Press), 1984, pp. 21–24.

9. Texas Comptroller of Public Accounts, *Fiscal Notes* (July 1994), p. 1.

10. Dallas County Community College District Telecourse, Government by Consent, "A Texas Perspective, Lesson One, Texas: Its Land and People, 1990."

11. Texas Comptroller of Public Accounts, *Texas: Where We Stand* (April 2003).

12. Texas Comptroller of Public Accounts, *Fiscal Notes* (Jan. 1994), p. 9.

13. Kirkpatrick Sale, *Power Shift* (New York: Random House), 1975, p. 48.

14. Texas Comptroller of Public Accounts, *Fiscal Notes* (Jan. 1994), p. 10.

15. Texas Comptroller of Public Accounts, *Fiscal Notes* (Nov. 1993), p. 1.

16. Morgan Quinto Corporation, *State Rankings 2001: A Statistical View of the Fifty States*.

17. Texas Comptroller of Public Accounts, *Fiscal Notes* (May 1994), pp. 8–9.

18. Texas Comptroller of Public Accounts, *Fiscal Notes* (April 1994), p. 1.

19. Texas Comptroller of Public Accounts, *The Changing Face of Texas* (August 1992), p. 5.

20. Texas Comptroller of Public Accounts, *The Changing Face of Texas* (August 1992), p. 6.

21. Peter Maass, "The Breaking Point," *New York Times Magazine* (August 21, 2005).

22. Jan Jarboe, "Gone to Texas," *Texas Monthly* (February 1993), p. 172.

2

The Constitution

INTRODUCTION

The basic purpose of a written constitution is to establish the institutions of government and to define their relationships with each other, with other governments, and with the governed. In other words, a constitution *limits* government. In the United States, written constitutions have been basic to the structure and function of national, state, and city governments since the American Revolution. However, the true character of a government is determined not by the provisions of its constitution, but by its political environment. Although our national, state, and local governments might be vastly different were it not for their constitutions, it is the people, especially politically influential people, who truly affect government. Thus, government is more than the structure described in its constitution; it is a process of decision making. This process results from the interaction of many environmental factors, including history, culture, the economy, social problems, attitudes, societal myths, folkways and taboos, and the complexity of pressures brought to bear by interest groups and political activists.

Still, a constitution must be composed of many important political elements because it establishes the basic rules by which the political game is played, and in doing so strongly influences who the winners will be when political conflict occurs. Thus, the decisions made by the writers of a constitution directly affect future political decisions. These choices establish a government, assign power to its various structures, and place limits on the exercise of that power. They also create a document that must guide the actions taken by courts, legislatures, executives, interest groups, and even the people themselves.

TEXAS IN THE FEDERAL SYSTEM

The authority of Texas government is limited by the larger system in which it operates. When Texas joined the United States in 1845, it was joining a federal system of government. The U.S. Constitution created the federal system by allocating power between two levels of government, state and national. Although the relationship between the national and state governments has evolved over the years, a constitutional division of powers remains the essential feature of the federal system.

DIVISION OF POWERS

National Powers

Delegated   The powers granted to the national government in the U.S. Constitution, listed in Articles 1, 2, 3, and especially Article 1, Section 8, are called delegated powers.

Implied   In the Supreme Court case *McCulloch v. Maryland* (1819), Chief Justice John Marshall ruled that because of the "necessary and proper" clause in Article 1, Section 8, the national government had additional powers that were implied in that clause.

Concurrent Powers

Usually, delegated powers can only be used by the national government, but both levels of government share some of these powers. The powers shared by state and national governments are called concurrent powers. Some examples of these powers are the power to tax, the power to borrow, and the power to regulate commerce within their own areas of authority.

Reserved Powers

The most significant reserved power given to states by the U.S. Constitution is the power to determine the qualifications for voting (see Chapter 3 for a full discussion). The U.S. Constitution itself does not outline other areas of a state's authority. The Tenth Amendment to the U.S. Constitution does read: "The powers not delegated to the United States by the Constitution, not prohibited by it to the States, are **reserved** to the States or to the people." From this amendment, state powers are called reserved powers. The courts have generally interpreted that "reserved" powers of the states fall into three main areas. The first is public education, which is the single largest area of expenditure for most states. Second, police powers are the responsibility of the state. Most crimes in this country are determined by state penal codes, which can vary among states. For example, some states, such as Texas, impose capital punishment for certain crimes as a part of their penal code, while other states do not. Finally, the right to regulate commerce within a state, intrastate commerce, remains with the state government. In Texas, the Texas Railroad Commission and the Texas Department of Commerce regulate many areas of intrastate commerce.

HORIZONTAL FEDERALISM

In addition to having a relationship with the national government in a federal system, the state of Texas also has a relationship with all the other states in the system. This kind of relationship is usually referred to as horizontal federalism. Article 4 of the U.S. Constitution describes the basic relationships between states in Section 1, "Full Faith and Credit," and Section 2, "Privileges and Immunities." In Section 1, the concept is that each state must accept other states' public acts, records, and judicial proceedings. For example, a divorce decree granted in one state must be accepted as valid by the other states. Section 2 means that citizens are granted the same rights and duties, no matter in what state they reside. For example, jury duty is a responsibility that citizens have in all states. This section also contains the provision of interstate extradition, in which individuals accused of felony crimes can be returned to the state from which they fled in order to stand trial.

SUPREMACY CLAUSE

Article 6 of the U.S. Constitution makes it clear that whenever state and national laws conflict, the national law is supreme. Although each level of government (national or state) has its own areas of authority, national law prevails in the event of conflict. This is the final feature of our federal system.

STATE CONSTITUTIONS

The Politics of Political Change

There have been many fundamental changes in the character of our federal system of government since its inception. The national government has grown significantly in power, while at the same time increasing its protection of democracy and certain other concepts of liberty. Yet most of these changes have been accomplished with few formal amendments to the U.S. Constitution. The Constitution only deals with the most basic elements of government, leaving most decisions to Congress, the president, and the courts. Because it does not lock government into a rigid framework, it has been able to sustain mammoth fundamental changes in government and society with only twenty-seven formal amendments.

In contrast, state constitutions are not only much longer than the national constitution, but frequently they deal with the details of both governmental structure and policy. Too often, they try to solve problems and establish policies rather than simply delegating authority to the appropriate people and institutions.[1] Consequently, as changing political and social conditions require changes in government structure and policy, formal constitutional amendments are necessary. There are several reasons for these frequent amendments.

1. A state's constitution is the basic law of the state, but interest groups and voters seem to view it as more than this: They fail to make clear distinctions between *what ought to be* and *what ought to be in the constitution,* And consequently, all sorts of details creep into the document.

2. Institutions and interest groups frequently feel safer when their interests are protected in the constitution, because it is more difficult to change than ordinary law. Thus, state constitutions contain lengthy and detailed protection for vested interests.

3. State governments have a peculiar position in the federal system. When the colonies declared their independence from Britain, the newly created states were assumed to have all the domestic powers that had previously been exercised by the Crown. States do not have governments of "delegated" powers, but are presumed to have all the powers that have not been explicitly prohibited them. Thus, citizens fearing strong governments have felt the need to place detailed constitutional restrictions on state governments.

4. When state governments misuse their powers, the response from the citizenry is usually to deny them such powers. These limitations and restrictions add immensely to the length of state constitutions (although there is serious doubt that they add much responsibility to government).

5. State constitutions are poorly written and arranged. Some provisions are so badly drafted that they are interpreted to be even more restrictive than the constitution's framers probably intended.

Although the constitutions of some states (Alaska and Hawaii are two) are rather concise and seldom need amending, most states have had to completely rewrite their constitutions. The constitution of Texas is over 130 years old, contains almost 80,000 words, and has been amended 432 times as of 2002 (see Figure 2.1).

The continual amendment of detailed and restrictive state constitutions means that citizens are frequently called on to pass judgment on the proposed amendments. Theoretically, this gives the electorate popular control of government; however, low voter turnout for constitutional elections seems to indicate that there

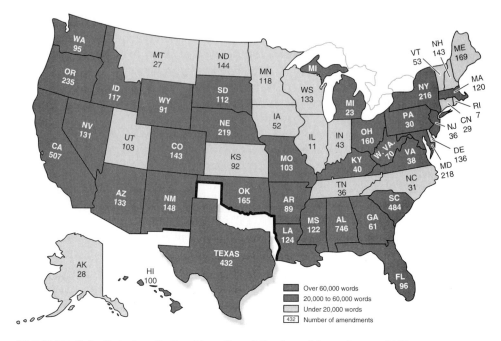

FIGURE 2.1 State Constitutions' Length and Number of Amendments, 2002

SOURCE: Data from *The Book of the States 2002*, p. 14, Council of State Governments. *Delegates to the Constitutional Convention of 1875.* Courtesy of Prints and Photographs Collection, The Center for American History, The University of Texas at Austin, CN01063.

is little voter interest in exercising popular control through the amendment process. The average citizen, faced with confusing, technical, or trivial amendments, simply does not participate. Still, constitutions are frequently revised, and therefore reflect the political climate more accurately than does the U.S. Constitution. These amendments can be seen as historical records of the waves of political change that have moved across the nation. (See page 32 for an update on the latest Texas Constitution amendments.)

State Constitutions in History

The First State Constitutions   The first state constitutions, developed from colonial charters, reflected the new political realities that followed the revolution. The colonists had experienced much abuse of executive power under King George III and his appointed governors, so the earliest state constitutions adhered to the idea of legislative supremacy. Because the most representative colonial institutions had been the colonial assemblies, state legislatures usually were given not only the power to select the governor and the judges, but to make virtually every important decision of government. Thus, the earliest state governments did not provide for any real separation of governmental powers.

Pre-Civil War Democracy   During the nineteenth century, as America continued to wrestle with the ideals of democracy, states were forced to lower suffrage requirements and offer the electorate a larger voice in the decisions of government. Americans discovered that executive offices could also serve as instruments of democracy, and state constitutions began to provide for the election of governors and, as the role of state government grew, other executive officers. However, executive power was often divided among several elected officials, demonstrating a lingering fear of the executive branch of government, which continues even today in most states, including Texas.

Nevertheless, the independent election of executive officials marked the beginning of the separation of state governments' powers and the opportunity to check their legislatures, which remained the superior branches of government. As democracy continued to take deeper root, judges also were elected. The *long ballot,* which provides for the direct election of numerous executive and court officials, had its origins in the era of Jacksonian Democracy—an era that would later affect the structure of Texas government.

The search for true democracy permeated virtually every aspect of political life. Political parties rushed to organize the large mass of newly enfranchised voters and established the *spoils system:* the hiring of loyal party members for government jobs once the party was in power. Knowing that the next election could sweep them from their jobs if the opposition won, these government employees began to take advantage of whatever opportunity arose for their own private gain. Insecurity in public employment led to corruption, which in turn led to political bosses and machine politics. Later, the mass immigration of people from Eastern Europe to the big cities of the North and East gave a boost to the power and effectiveness of political machines in those areas.

Correcting Abuses   In many ways, the latter half of the nineteenth century might be called the Dark Ages of American democracy. Following the Civil War, the Reconstruction governments of the Southern states, selected by undemocratic means, were abusive, corrupt, and had little experience in public affairs. Despite a few forward-looking policies proposed by these governments (particularly in the area of education), Southerners generally could see only their negative aspects. When free elections were again instituted in the South, Southerners systematically scrapped the policies implemented by the Reconstruction governments.

But misuse of power was not confined to the Southern states. Industrialization in the North produced economic magnates—the robber barons—who dominated state governments even more easily than they did the national government. At the same time, this post-Civil War industrialization attracted increasing waves of European immigrants, who, in turn, reinforced the power of the corrupt municipal political machines, as the machines offered jobs or food and drink at election time. because these incompetent and corrupt governments could not deal effectively with the problems of industrialization, urban growth, and increased demand for government services, undercurrents of reform began to stir. Paranoia, racism, and nativism fed these reform movements, which in the urban North demanded the destruction of immigrant-supported political machines. In the rural South (including Texas), the widespread reaction against the corruption and abuses of Reconstruction governments was increased and worsened by racism and hatred of the governments that had treated African Americans so well.

Reform took several directions. Some states (not Texas) adopted civil service measures to replace the old spoils system. Texas and several other states attempted to take politics out of public administration by establishing appointed boards of citizens to oversee administrative agencies and departments. Constitutional limitation on legislative power was another attempt to curtail corruption. These reforms included a whole host of details that could only be changed through constitutional amendment. The statutory detail found in most state constitutions refutes the faith that the people of an earlier era had in their legislative bodies, which they regarded as reliable reservoirs of the public trust.

Reform movements of the twentieth century added a new twist: Rather than simply limiting governmental power, efforts have been made to make it more democratic. For example, during the first few decades of the twentieth century, states adopted the direct primary system (rather than relying on conventions) to nominate candidates for office, though political parties continue to nominate their candidates for president and vice president in convention.

Probably few of the abuses of the nineteenth century were cured by the prescriptions of reformers, however. City machines began to crumble because citizens became more educated and government services became too complex for machine appointees to handle. Franklin Roosevelt's New Deal made social assistance a national policy rather than a favor of the city machine. At the same time, robber barons developed more subtle techniques to control the economy so that their heavy-handed influence seemed to diminish. Increased governmental regulation of the economy also made it seem that concentrations of private wealth could no longer be used for obviously selfish ends.

THE TEXAS CONSTITUTION

The Texas Constitution in History

1827   Even before there was a Texas Constitution, Texans, as Mexican citizens, lived under constitutional government. The Mexican Federal Constitution of 1824 and the Coahuila y Tejas Constitution of 1827 shaped the course of history, which led to a separation from Mexico and the establishment of a Texas Republic. Aspects of this constitution remain in the Texas Constitution today in property and land laws, water laws and water rights, and community property.

Whether the central government power was located in Mexico City; Austin, Texas; Richmond, Virginia; or Washington, D.C., Texans have a long history of being suspicious of giving too much power to government. As in other states, Texas's constitutional development reflects the interests and concerns of those who have written and amended it. Many of its changes parallel those of other states' constitutions; some are unique to Texas. Texans have lived under six other constitutions since separating from Mexico.[2]

1836   The 1836 constitution, which was written for the Republic of Texas, included features similar to the U.S. Constitution and the constitutions of Southern states. There were also some elements from Spanish political culture due to the influence of Jose Antonio Navarro, one of the two native Texans at the constitutional convention. One of the most significant features of this constitution was the legalization of slavery and the free importation of slaves from the United States. This pro-slavery action in 1836 delayed Texas's annexation into the United States and set into motion forces that would lead to Texas's secession from the Union during the Civil War. It would also have a direct impact on the present Texas constitution.

1845   On December 29, 1845, Texas officially became the twenty-eighth state in the union. Several articles of annexation were more or less peculiar to Texas. Most important of these was that Texas retained ownership of its public lands, which allowed the educational endowments made by the state to public education, mentioned in Chapter 1. The annexation articles also granted a historical oddity, which would be impossible to use today. Texas was given the right to divide itself into as many as five states. This agreement was an attempt by Congress to keep a balanced ratio of slave and free states in the United States, so that representation in the U.S. Senate would be balanced.

The main changes in this constitution, compared with the 1836 constitution, were the addition of an entire section on education and an expanded Bill of Rights, which was moved from the back of the constitution to the front.

1861   Although Sam Houston, Texas founder, hero, senator, and later governor, was opposed to secession from the Union, the secession ordinance was approved by popular vote in 1861. The 1861 constitution, which reflected this new reality, was simply the 1845 constitution amended to fit the circumstances. All references to "the United States" were deleted or replaced with "the Confederate States." Texas became a state in the Confederate States of America (CSA). (A confederation is a loose collection of sovereign states.) In 1869, the U.S. Supreme Court ruled in the case of *Texas v. White* that states cannot secede from the Union.

1866   Following the end of the Civil War and collapse of the Confederacy, relative anarchy existed in Texas until it was occupied and put under the military rule of the U.S. Army. General Philip Sheridan was the military governor of Louisiana and Texas from 1865 to 1868. His attitude toward Texas was expressed in his famous quote, "If I owned both Hell and Texas, I'd rent out Texas and live in Hell." The constitution of 1866 made only limited concessions to the defeat of the Confederacy in the Civil War. This constitution was never put into effect, and military rule continued in Texas until political authorities could write a suitable constitution.

1869   In 1868, the military rulers of Texas gave political leaders another chance to write an acceptable constitution. Anyone who had in any way supported the Confederacy was disqualified from voting. As a result, radical Republican politicians wrote the 1869 constitution. This constitution did ensure the readmission of Texas to the Union and the end of military occupation, but it centralized state government, weakened local governments, and provided for a strong, four-year-term governor and high salaries for public officials. The governor was given the power to appoint the judges, and it was determined that the legislature would meet in annual sessions. This document reflected little of the fear of governmental power that was later to become the hallmark of Texas government, and it was a document that former Confederate sympathizers would reject as soon as possible.

The constitution of 1869 served as the instrument of government for an era that some Texans regard as the most corrupt and abusive in the state's history. Under Republican governor E. J. Davis, large gifts of public funds were made to various interests such as the railroads, tax rates skyrocketed to pay for ambitious public programs, landowners refused to pay high taxes, and government accumulated what was an incredible public debt for that day. By using the state police and militia to maintain control, Governor Davis came to symbolize big government. He took control of voter registration, intimidated newspapers that were unfavorable to his policies, and arrested political opponents. His last act in office was to have his handpicked Supreme Court rule that the placement of a semi-colon invalidated the election of Democrat Richard Coke. Then, unwilling to give up his office, Davis surrounded himself with armed state police on the ground floor of the capitol building as the Democrats moved in upstairs to begin the organization of a new government. Davis finally gave up his office when the Texas militia turned against him.

1876   Recent scholarship has determined that Governor Davis did not abuse his powers to the extent previously believed. In fact, his administration had some positive programs. He built the foundation of a public school system, built roads, and passed a homestead law. Nevertheless, for Texans of the day, Reconstruction left a bitter memory of a humiliating, corrupt, and extravagant government. The ninety delegates to the constitutional convention of 1875, for the most part, Democrats who were determined to strike at the heart of the "big government" that had served Reconstruction. The convention constructed a constitution that cut the salaries of governing officials, placed strict limits on property taxes, restricted state borrowing, and eliminated the road tax. The term of office and the salary of the governor were reduced.

The "small government" bent of the convention also affected the legislature. Regular annual legislative sessions were limited to odd-numbered years, and each session was strictly limited in length. Legislative procedure was detailed in the constitution, and severe restrictions were placed on the kinds of policies the legislature might enact. As a restrictive measure, a number of public policies were written into the constitution, local government was revived, and counties were given most of the administrative and judicial functions of the state.

In spite of opposition from African Americans, Republicans, and railroad interests, the new state constitution was ratified in the 1876 election. The 1876 constitution is the current constitution, which will be examined in some detail.

Delegates to the Constitutional Convention of 1875

The Texas Constitution Today

Students often study state constitutions with an ideal or model constitution in mind, and they are frequently left with the feeling that if only this or that constitutional provision were changed, state governments somehow would become honest, efficient, and effective. Such an impression is false. There is no ideal constitution that can adequately serve the diverse and unique political cultures of all fifty states. And there is no single state constitution that, unchanged, could permanently meet the fluctuating needs and concerns of its citizens. Moreover, as stated earlier, government is much more than its constitution. Honest and effective government is the result of the political environment—the attitudes of elected leaders, party officials, interest-group leaders, and ordinary citizens.

A state constitution is not incidental to good government, however. Low salaries established by the constitution may discourage independent, high-caliber leaders from seeking office; constitutional restrictions may make it virtually impossible for government to meet the changing needs of its citizenry; institutions may be established in such a way that they will be unresponsive and will operate inefficiently. Thus, a workable constitution is a prerequisite for good government.

The events of the decade prior to 1876 created an environment in which a constitution capable of serving well under the pressures and changes that would take place in the century to follow could not be written. Consequently, solutions to the problems of the 1870s are often locked into a document that now has to serve the twenty-first century.

Basic Characteristics   The current Texas Constitution has three fundamental characteristics, which will become apparent as we review the document article by article.

1.   The document's main purpose is to restrict the power and authority of the government. The Texas political culture of individualism and traditionalism supports the idea of a government limited to basic essential functions. The societal anger about Reconstruction and military rule in Texas added emphasis to the idea of restricting the power of government institutions and officials.

2.   The constitution contains an excessive amount of detail. Some authors maintain that the Texas Constitution is not really a constitution, which is supposed to provide a broad flexible framework for government, but a legislative code. A legislative code contains detailed provisions that the legislative branch would otherwise be creating on a year-by-year basis. As a result of putting excessive detail in a document from the 1870s, the Texas constitution is guaranteed to become quickly outdated and obsolete. This leads directly to the final characteristic.

3.   The Texas Constitution has had to be amended frequently. As mentioned earlier, the Texas Constitution has been amended 432 times. Often, amendments make the constitution more difficult to read and understand.

The frequent amending and the fact that the constitution is poorly written have made the constitution even more restrictive than the writers in 1875 probably intended.

Basic Constitutional Articles

The Bill of Rights   Like every other state constitution, the constitution of Texas reflects a basic principle in American political culture—that government ought to be limited. Article 1 of the constitution—the Bill of Rights—contains the most basic of these limitations on Texas government. Many provisions in the state Bill of Rights are also protected against state action by the Fourteenth Amendment to the U.S. Constitution—freedom of expression and religion and fair play for those accused of crimes. The Texas constitution also guarantees rights not included in the U.S. Constitution. For example, Texas has a provision to prohibit discrimination based on sex. The Equal Rights Amendment to the U.S. Constitution was similar, but was never ratified by the required number of states. The Texas Bill of Rights also forbids committing the mentally ill for an extended period without a jury trial, and prohibits the suspending of the writ of *habeas corpus* under *any* circumstances.

Separation of Powers   Article 2 provides for a "separation of powers." To prevent the concentration of power in the hands of any single institution, the federal government, as well as every state, has divided government's functions among three branches: the legislative, the executive, and the judicial.

However, because at the time of the constitution's inception there was still the potential for any of these three branches to abuse the powers they had been granted, Texas's Constitution followed American tradition and established a system of checks and balances, whereby one branch was permitted to intervene in certain functions assigned to another branch. For example, the governor becomes involved in the legislative process when he or she vetoes legislation, while the senate must confirm the governor's appointments.

THE LEGISLATIVE BRANCH   Most legislative power is assigned to a two-house (bicameral) legislative body. However, the legislative article (Article 3) does more than just define the general functions and membership of the legislature.

1. It requires a majority of voters to change legislators' $7,200 annual salary.

2. Rather than allowing the legislature to set its own rules of procedure, the constitution provides, among other procedural stipulations, that unless four-fifths of the membership is in agreement, legislation must be read on three separate days before it can be enacted.

3. It provides for relatively short, regular legislative sessions (140 days) and limits regular sessions to odd-numbered years.

4. It severely limits legislative power—for example, the legislature cannot authorize borrowing, although bonds can be sold.

5. It makes policy in a variety of other areas that would normally be made by a statute enacted by the legislature.

Such details in the constitution mean that amendments are necessary to change relatively unimportant decisions that could otherwise easily be changed by the legislature or delegated to state bureaucrats.

THE EXECUTIVE BRANCH   Although Article 4 provides that the governor shall be the "chief executive," it actually divides the executive powers among a number of independently elected executive officers. The legislature has reinforced this *plural executive* system by making most administrative agencies independent of real control by the governor. In fact, if the governor is an effective leader, it is in spite of the Texas Constitution. One major detrimental effect of this fragmentation of state government is that it blurs the lines of administrative responsibility. The governor does, however, have the item veto power to strike out parts of an appropriation bill without vetoing the entire legislation.

THE COURTS   The constitution also fragments the court system. Texas has two separate courts of final appeal—one for civil matters (the Texas Supreme Court) and one for criminal matters (the Court of Criminal Appeals). The numerous high and lower courts are confusing to the average citizen.

State courts, too, have come under attack because they lack qualified judges. For example, the constitution specifies only general qualifications for justices of the peace; they need not be qualified lawyers or judges. Although in a simpler, rural setting there may have been good reason for laypersons to serve as judges, today those most familiar with court operations regard this viewpoint as an anachronism.

The manner of selecting judges also affects their qualifications. All judges provided for in the constitution are elected to four- or six-year terms. Most states elect their judges, but many scholars regard this effort at popular control as undesirable; judges may become too dependent on campaign contributions from attorneys to apply the law in a uniform and even-handed manner.

Local Government   The constitution provides for a substantial amount of power to be executed at the local level, especially within the county. Yet the writers of the constitution, reacting to the abuses of the highly centralized Reconstruction government, showed a distrust even of county governments by stipulating a structure for them in which administrative power and authority are divided and diffused.

In contrast to the rigid limitations on county governmental organization, the constitution is much more flexible regarding municipal governments. The legislature, which has the power to establish structures for city governments, has offered municipalities several alternative "general law" charters. Cities with a population over 5,000 may adopt home-rule charters of their own. Cities may adopt any program that does not conflict with state law or the constitution; only taxation limitations restrict city government.

Generally, the legislature has the power to provide for the establishment of limited-purpose local governments, known as special districts. A number of special districts, such as water, hospital, and road, are also authorized by the constitution.

Suffrage   A major function of the states is to determine the character of democracy in America as they set suffrage requirements and administer elections. Article 6 of the Texas Constitution establishes suffrage requirements. The U.S. Supreme Court, however, has found many of the provisions of this article to be in violation of the U.S. Constitution—for example, the stipulation that a voter must own taxable property in order to vote in bond elections. Other provisions have been superseded by amendments to the U.S. Constitution—for example, the proviso that a voter is at least twenty-one years of age.

Amendments   As is true of other constitutions, amendment of the Texas Constitution requires two steps: proposal and ratification. Two-thirds of the entire membership of each house in the Texas legislature must vote to propose an amendment. To put the amendment into effect, ratification requires approval by a majority of voters in a general or special election. Although Texas makes it more difficult to amend its constitution than do most states, only a few states have amended their constitutions more frequently.

Evaluating the Texas Constitution

The reactions of Texans to Reconstruction led to the adoption of a constitution whose major object was to curb governmental power. Thus, the governmental institutions that it establishes are decentralized, with their powers dispersed, and rigid, restrictive constitutional limitations are placed on routine governmental procedures and activities. Several adverse effects arise from such restrictions.

1. It is difficult for state government to develop significantly, to change or institute effective policy, without first amending the constitution.
2. The division of executive power makes it very difficult for the governor or any other public official to become an effective leader.
3. Diffusion of executive and judicial powers means that most units of government function with little or no supervision. Yet, because of the bewildering conglomeration of courts and agencies, voters tend to hold officials in the more visible public offices responsible for policies over which they really have little or no control.

The constitution itself is a source of confusion, containing descriptions of most of the fundamentals of government and detailing provisions concerning matters that might better be left to the ongoing institutions of government. A constitution should include only *organic law;* that is, it should organize responsible institutions of government. The Texas Constitution is poorly written. Not only is there great ambiguity and overlap, but it is also poorly organized. This has led to a restrictive interpretation of its provisions and, as an

FIGURE 2.2 Statutory Initiative and Referendum and Recall in the States.
SOURCE: Data from *The Book of the States 2002*, pp. 223, 248–249, Council of State Governments.

unreadable document, it promotes ignorance of its contents and confusion as to its intentions.

1974 Constitutional Convention   With all the restrictions on government power that have been written into the Texas Constitution, supposedly to protect citizens, it is interesting that the 1876 constitution does not allow provisions that the voters of many other states have. These provisions are initiative and recall. In other words, citizens cannot directly take action to amend the constitution or vote officials out of office before their term is up. Only the members of the Texas legislature can propose constitutional change (see Figure 2.2).

Public pressure led by government scholars and the League of Women Voters organization finally resulted in action. In 1972, the Texas legislature proposed an amendment calling for a vote on holding a constitutional convention to write a modern constitution, to be held in 1974. The voters of Texas overwhelmingly approved this amendment.

Under the provisions of the amendment, a Constitutional Revision Commission was established to hold public hearings and to submit a model constitution proposal to the constitutional convention. Another important provision was for the members of the legislature to serve as the delegates to the convention. The convention met and worked for months attempting to write a modern constitution. The convention, however, was divided over the issue of a right-to-work provision to restrict labor unions and failed by three votes to muster the necessary two-thirds vote to submit the document to the voters to be ratified.

The Texas legislature proposed new amendments to the constitution to try to salvage the efforts of the Revision Commission. The election for the new amendments was held in November 1975. Opposition to change was very strong. In an emotional appeal, opponents of the new constitution raised three major issues. First, they said the new constitution gave too much power to the legislature. Second, they claimed the new constitution would raise the costs of government. Third, they said the new constitution could bring the possibility of a state income tax. All of these charges would certainly be concepts that are in opposition to the beliefs of the Texas political culture.

The opponents spent much more money than the proponents. This money, when combined with an appeal to emotion—especially distrust of the legislature—as well as voter apathy and confusion, worked toward the defeat of the reforms. In the end, only 23 percent of registered voters cast ballots in the election, and they overwhelmingly rejected the amendments. As the victorious opponents of reform reminded Texans, "the Texas Constitution has survived the test of time."

Supporters of constitutional reform have since won some victories, as several of the changes that were proposed have been implemented as a result of court orders, statutes, and subsequent constitutional amendments.

CONCLUSION

The Texas Constitution had undergone piecemeal change in the decades of the 1980s and 1990s. The debacle of constitutional reform in the 1970s made it difficult for concerned groups to pressure for a new constitutional convention. The need for change is obvious, as the second most populous state in the United States continues to operate a legislature that meets in regular session only five months out of a two-year period.

Meaningful reform in the twenty-first century can only come about with the citizens' awareness of this problem, and their efforts in the political process. In November 2005 Texans will vote on nine more constitutional amendments, including the controversial amendment to prohibit gay marriage. In the next chapter, we will examine the opportunities for political participation.

KEY TERMS

Bill of Rights

concurrent powers

delegated powers

federalism

horizontal federalism

1974 constitutional
   convention

reserved powers

separation of powers

suffrage

supremacy clause

Logging On

The U.S. Constitution sets the context for the powers of the state of Texas in relationship to the national government and the other forty-nine states. See the U.S. Constitution, especially Articles 4 and 6, and the Tenth Amendment to the Constitution, at **http://www.law.cornell.edu/constitution/constitution.overview.html**.

The case of *McCulloch v. Maryland* (1819) was critical in establishing what powers the national government would have in relationship to state powers. See a summary and the actual text of the decision at **http://www.constitution.org/ussc/017-316_.htm**.

What you have all been waiting for, with all seventeen articles—the complete text of the Texas Constitution at **http://www.capitol.state.tx.us/txconst/toc.html**.

ENDNOTES

1. George D. Braden, *Citizens' Guide to the Texas Constitution* (University of Houston Institute for Urban Studies), 1972, p. 6.

2. Staff of the Institute of Texan Cultures, "Texas and Her Constitutions," *San Antonio Express-News,* June 2, 1974, pp. 1–36. The section on the Texas Constitution in History relies on this material.

3

Political Participation
and Elections

INTRODUCTION

One of the most significant powers given to states by the U.S. Constitution is the right to determine voting qualifications. Texas and other states have used this power to deny voting rights to Native Americans, African Americans, and women. Over the years, constitutional amendments, Supreme Court cases, and acts of Congress have greatly expanded the right to vote.

In spite of actions expanding the right to vote, voter turnout in Texas is lower than in most other states. This low level of participation is usually attributed to administrative factors such as voter registration, ballots and election administration in general, and socioeconomic characteristics of the population.

The nomination of candidates to run for public office was originally limited to a small group of influential men called a caucus. As the right to vote expanded, the number of people able to nominate candidates also expanded. The primary election allowed the average person to nominate candidates for office. Today, there are primary elections, run-off elections, general elections, special elections, and nonpartisan city and special district elections. While this number and variety of elections may confuse the voter, it is important in a democracy to have a high level of participation at each election.

VOTING

Voting is one of the most—if not the most—important acts performed by citizens in a democracy. It allows citizens to choose between competing political parties in order to determine who their leaders will be. It gives government legitimacy by assuring citizens that the coalitions that gain control of the government have the right to make and enforce policy. Having the right to vote helps participants to feel that they are a part of the political system and thus have the right to try to bring about change. One example of this is the case of eighteen-year-olds who have been given the right to vote. Although this has had negligible effect on public policy due both to their low voter turnout and divided ideology, young people seem to feel that they are a part of the policy-making aspect of the system.

Voter Qualifications

Today it is easy to become a qualified voter in Texas. One must be (1) a citizen of the United States, (2) a resident of a Texas county thirty days prior to the election, and (3) eighteen years of age or older. Convicted felons are disqualified for two years after completing their sentence.

The official responsible for registration administration in Texas is the county tax assessor-collector or the county election administrator. The voter may register at any time during the year either in person or by mail, or through a spouse, parent, or child who is a registered voter. New voter registration certificates are mailed every two years, but the registration list is essentially permanent, because voters are removed from it only if the non-forwardable voter certificates are returned by mail.

Although Texas presently has very lenient requirements for voting, throughout most of the state's history the opposite has been true. Formally and informally, Texas systematically denied large segments of the population the right to participate in the electoral process. In fact, Texas had some of the most restrictive voting requirements in the nation.

Formal Restraints   Article 1, Section 2, in the U.S. Constitution reads, "The electors in each state shall have the qualifications requisite for electors of the most numerous Branch of the State Legislature." Thus, each state establishes its own criteria for voter qualification. Throughout much of the history of Texas, various laws and constitutional restraints have either directly prohibited or discouraged potential voters. A brief review will highlight the changes that have occurred in

U.S. constitutional amendments, Supreme Court decisions, and U.S. congressional action to extend voting rights.

The first major change in voting requirements came as a result of the passage of the Thirteenth, Fourteenth, and Fifteenth Amendments to the U.S. Constitution. These amendments, known as the Civil War Amendments, freed the slaves, protected their rights against state action, and allowed African American men the right to vote.

After Reconstruction and the end of military rule in the Southern states, state laws were used to prevent African American men from voting. A number of discriminatory laws for registration and voting were passed. Some of these laws called for literacy tests or constitutional interpretation tests in order to qualify to register to vote. Though many Anglo-American men could not pass these tests either, the grandfather clause was used to permit individuals to vote if their ancestors had been registered to vote prior to the adoption of the Fifteenth Amendment. The grandfather clause was ruled unconstitutional by the U.S. Supreme Court in the case of *Guinn v. U.S.* (1915). Texas never employed the grandfather clause or literacy tests, supposedly because the high level of illiteracy in the state would be revealed.

The poll tax was another major barrier to voting created by the state of Texas. This law, adopted in 1902, required a payment of $1.50 to $1.75 in order to register to vote. This law usually hit minority men harder than Anglo-Americans, but still kept a large number of poor Anglos from voting. The poll tax in Texas was usually coupled with a very restrictive annual voter registration. Citizens could only register each year between October 1 and January 31. The registration period began in the year before the election and lasted only four months.

In 1906, Texas developed the "white primary" as a means of limiting African American voting. The Democratic Party dominated almost all Southern states after the Civil War. To exclude African American men from the Democratic primary vote effectively gave them no voice in government. The U.S. Supreme Court ruled the white primary unconstitutional in a Texas case, *Smith v. Allwright* (1944).

The next great expansion of voting occurred in 1920, with the passage of the Nineteenth Amendment to the U.S. Constitution. This amendment gave women the right to vote. Another major expansion of voting rights occurred in 1971 with the passage of the Twenty-Sixth Amendment to the U.S. Constitution, allowing eighteen-year-old citizens to vote. The Twenty-Fourth Amendment to the U.S. Constitution in 1964 ended the poll tax for national elections. Later, in 1966, the U.S. Supreme Court ruled the poll-tax requirement in state elections unconstitutional in the case of *Harper v. Virginia Board of Elections.*

In spite of these constitutional changes and U.S. Supreme Court decisions, the U.S. Congress felt that state officials were still denying African Americans and other minorities the right to vote. The Voting Rights Act passed by Congress in 1965 brought African Americans into the voting population in record numbers by suspending state and county registration laws and, in some cases, using federal officials to register voters. The Voting Rights Act was amended and extended in 1970 and 1975. In 1975, Texas fell under the provisions of the act for the first time.

The state was required to print ballots in Spanish and English. This requirement caused bilingual voting information to be printed in parts of twenty-four states. In 1982, the Voting Rights Act was extended until 2007. For this time period, the U.S. Justice Department will monitor any changes in election laws that might adversely affect minority voters in states such as Texas. The debate over renewing the act has already begun in mostly Southern states.

Through U.S. constitutional amendments, various Supreme Court decisions, and the Voting Rights Act, legal or formal barriers to voting have largely been eliminated. However, there are still informal barriers, which are not easily changed.

Informal Restraints African Americans, Mexican Americans, and women were denied the right vote as much by informal means as by law. The threat of physical violence was used effectively throughout much of Texas to curtail minority voting, as was the threat of economic reprisal. As Anglos controlled the economic system throughout most of Texas, it became a simple and effective instrument for intimidating minorities. Thus, the fear of losing credit at the general store, being unable to receive a bank loan, or losing a job was usually enough to discourage voting, even when formal restraints had been removed.

The Texas political culture discussed in Chapter 1 is also an informal restraint on voting. Because Texas, according to Daniel Elazar, has a Traditionalistic and Individualistic political culture, participation is not encouraged among ordinary citizens. Upper- and middle-class citizens, who have the time and money, participate and compete in the electoral arena. This political culture is evolving as migrants from Moralistic political cultures come to Texas, but it still has a powerful influence on voting behavior.

ELECTION ADMINISTRATION

How state and local officials carry out their duties can also have a major impact on voting. The Voting Rights Act and amendments passed by Congress attempted to streamline this part of the voting process. In 1967, the Texas legislature designated the secretary of state as the chief elections officer of Texas. In this capacity, the secretary of state interprets legislation, issues guidelines, and distributes funds to local officials to run the primary elections. The secretary of state also makes sure that the state of Texas complies with the provisions of the U.S. Voting Rights Act.

Traditionally, both the county clerk and tax assessor-collector have had election responsibilities at the local level. The Texas legislature, to improve election efficiency, has provided an alternative organization that combines election duty functions in the county clerk's office.

In 1979, the legislature allowed counties to combine all elections-related duties of county officials into the single position of a county elections administrator, who is appointed for a two-year term by the County Elections Board.

Ballot Length

Another key element in election administration is the ballot itself. A government in which relatively few offices are filled by election has a *short ballot*. For example, for national government in the United States a single voter is called upon only to fill the offices of president, vice president, two senators, and one representative. All other officials are appointed.

Texas state and county governments provide classic examples of the *long ballot*. Texas's Constitution requires election of numerous executive and judicial officials, plus several legislators for both county and state governments.

Arguments against the short ballot usually conclude that filling positions by appointment would place too much power in the hands of the governor, county executive, or a single individual, and that the only way government can remain democratic is through the popular election of its officials. Those in favor of the short ballot usually argue that it allows the people to place responsibility for government action on a relatively few officials. They further argue that the short ballot enables the average voter to vote intelligently for a few candidates, instead of being overwhelmed by the vast number of candidates on the long ballot. It becomes difficult to even remember the names of the elected officials, legislators, and judges, and thus, almost impossible to vote intelligently on their capabilities.

Ballot Construction

Two basic types of ballots are the *office-block* ballot and the *party-column* ballot. The office-block ballot lists candidates randomly under the office that they are seeking. This forces voters to look at the candidates for all parties for each office. This ballot emphasizes the office rather than the party and makes it more difficult to vote a straight party ticket. It therefore encourages *split ticket voting,* or voting for the candidate of one party for one office and the candidate of another party for another office.

The party-column ballot is used in Texas. As can be seen in Figure 3.1, on this ballot the offices are listed to the extreme left. Each candidate is listed in a column under his or her party and is placed to the right of the office sought. This ballot encourages *straight ticket voting:* All the voter has to do is mark one X (on a paper ballot) or pull one lever (on a voting machine) by the party name, and a vote will be recorded for all nominees of that party. This is a holdover from the days of one-party (Democrat) rule in Texas following the Civil War. Today, many voters tend to vote a split ticket, even with the party–column ballot.

Voter Participation

With these formal and informal restraints on voting in Texas, it is not surprising to discover that Texas has a very low voter turnout when compared with other states. Consistently, Texas has ranked from forty-fourth to forty-sixth in the last four presidential elections. The highest turnout was in 1992, with 49.1 percent of the voting-age population casting ballots. This was probably an ideal election for

BEXAR COUNTY JOINT GENERAL ELECTION
ELECCION JUNTA GENERAL CONDADO DE BEXAR

EDWARDS AQUIFER AUTHORITY - DISTRICTS 3 AND 7
AUTORIDAD DE AQUIFERO EDWARDS - DISTRITOS 3 & 7

TUESDAY, NOVEMBER 3, 1998
(MARTES 3 DE NOVIEMBRE DE 1998)

BEXAR METROPOLITAN WATER DISTRICT - DISTRICT 6
DISTRITO DE AGUA METROPOLITAN DE BEXAR - DISTRITO 6

SAMPLE BALLOT *(BOLETA DE MUESTRA)*

INSTRUCTION NOTE: Vote for the candidate of your choice in each race by placing an "X" in the square beside the candidate's name. You may cast a straight-party vote (that is, cast a vote for all the nominees of one party) by placing an "X" in the square beside the name of the party of your choice. If you cast a straight-party vote for all the nominees of one party and also cast a vote for an opponent of one of that party's nominees, your vote for the opponent will be counted as well as your vote for all the other nominees of the party for which the straight-party vote was cast.
(NOTA DE INSTRUCCION: Vote por el candidato de su preferencia para cada candidatura marcando una 'X' en el espacio cuadrado a la izquierda del nombre del candidato. Usted podrá votar por todos los candidatos de un solo partido político ('straight-ticket') marcando una 'X' en el espacio cuadrado a la izquierda del nombre de ese partido político. Si usted vota por uno de los partidos políticos y también vota por el contrincante de uno de los candidatos de dicho partido político, se contará su voto por el contrincante tanto como su voto por todos los demás candidatos del partido político de su preferencia.)

Candidates for: (Candidatos para:)	Republican Party (Partido Republicano)	Democratic Party (Partido Democratico)	Libertarian Party (Partido Liobertariano)	Independent (Independente)	Write-In (Voto Escrito)
Straight Party (Partido Completo)	☐ Republican (Republicano) (Rep)	☐ Democratic (Democrático) (Dem)	☐ Libertarian (Libertariano)		
United States Representative, District 20 (Representante de los Estados Unidos, Distrito Núm. 20)	☐ James Walker	☐ Charlie Gonzalez	☐ Alejandro (Alex) DePeña		
United States Representative, District 21 (Representante de los Estados Unidos, Distrito Núm. 21)	☐ Lamar Smith		☐ Jeffrey Charles Blunt		
United States Representative, District 23 (Representante de los Estados Unidos, Distrito Núm. 23)	☐ Henry Bonilla	☐ Charlie Urbina Jones	☐ William A. (Bill) Stallknecht		
United States Representative, District 28 (Representante de los Estados Unidos, Distrito Núm. 28)		☐ Ciro D. Rodriguez	☐ Edward Elmer		
Governor (Gobernador)	☐ George W. Bush	☐ Garry Mauro	☐ Lester R. "Les" Turlington, Jr.		☐ _____
Lieutenant Governor (Gobernador Teniente)	☐ Rick Perry	☐ John Sharp	☐ Anthony García		
Attorney General (Procurador General)	☐ John Cornyn	☐ Jim Mattox	☐ Mike Angwin		
Comptroller of Public Accounts (Contralor de Cuentas Públicas)	☐ Carole Keeton Rylander	☐ Paul Hobby	☐ Alex Monchak		
Commissioner of the General Land Office (Comisionado de la Oficina General de Terrenos)	☐ David Dewhurst	☐ Richard Raymond	☐ J. Manuel "Monte" Montez		
Commissioner of Agriculture (Comisionado de Argicultura)	☐ Susan Combs	☐ L.P. (Pete) Patterson	☐ Jimmy T. LaBaume		☐ _____
Railroad Commissioner (Comisionado de Ferrocarriles)	☐ Tony Garza	☐ Joe B. Henderson	☐ Jim Spurlock		
Justice, Supreme Court, Place 1 (Juez, Corte Suprema, Lugar Núm. 1)	☐ Craig T. Enoch	☐ Mike Westergren			
Justice, Supreme Court, Place 2 (Juez, Corte Suprema, Lugar Núm. 2)	☐ Harriet O'Neill	☐ Rose Spector			
Justice, Supreme Court, Place 3 (Juez, Corte Suprema, Lugar Núm. 3)	☐ Greg Abbott	☐ David Van Os			
Justice, Supreme Court, Place 4, Unexpired Term (Juez, Corte Suprema, Lugar Núm 4, Duración Restante del Cargo)	☐ Deborah Hankinson	☐ Jerry Scarbrough			
Judge, Court of Criminal Appeals, Place 1 (Juez, Corte de Apelaciones Criminales, Lugar Núm. 1)	☐ Mike Keasler	☐ Charles F. (Charlie) Baird			
Judge, Court of Criminal Appeals, Place 2 (Juez, Corte de Apelaciones Criminales, Lugar Núm. 2)	☐ Cheryl Johnson	☐ Winston Cochran			
Judge, Court of Criminal Appeals, Place 3 (Juez, Corte de Apelaciones Criminales, Lugar Núm. 3)	☐ Lawrence 'Larry' Meyers		☐ Larry S. Perry		
State Senator, District 19 (Senador Estatal, Distito Núm 19)		☐ Frank Madla			
State Representative, District 115 (Senador Estatal, Distrito Núm 115)		☐ Leticia Van de Putte			
State Representative, District 116 (Senador Estatal, Distrito Núm 116)		☐ Leo Alvarado, Jr.			
State Representative, District 117 (Senador Estatal, Distrito Núm 117)		☐ John Amos Longoria			
State Representative, District 118 (Senador Estatal, Distrito Núm 118)		☐ Carlos "Charlie" Uresti			
State Representative, District 119 (Senador Estatal, Distrito Núm 119)		☐ Robert Puente			
State Representative, District 120 (Senador Estatal, Distrito Núm 120)		☐ Ruth Jones McClendon			
State Representative, District 121 (Senador Estatal, Distrito Núm 121)	☐ Bill Siebert				
State Representative, District 122 (Senador Estatal, Distrito Núm 122)	☐ John H. Shields				
State Representative, District 123 (Senador Estatal, Distrito Núm 123)	☐ Frank J. Corte, Jr.				
State Representative, District 124 (Senador Estatal, Distrito Núm 124)		☐ Juan F. Solis, III			
State Representative, District 125 (Senador Estatal, Distrito Núm 125)		☐ Arthur "Art" Reyna			
Justice, 4th Court of Appeals, place 1 (Juez, Corte de Apelaciones, Distrito Núm 4)	☐ Tom Rickhoff				
Justice, 4th Court of Appeals, place 2, Unexpired Term (Juez, Corte de Apelaciones, Distrito Núm 2, Duración Restante del Cargo)	☐ Karen Angelini	☐ Jim Branton			
District Judge, 45th Judicial District (Juez del Distrito, Distrito Núm 45)	☐ Jim Brister	☐ Carol R. Haberman			

F I G U R E 3.1 Sample General Election Ballot

T A B L E 3.1 Percentage of Voter Turnout in Presidential Elections 1972–2004

	1972	1976	1980	1984	1988	1992	1996	2000	2004
U.S. Average	55.5	53.3	52.6	53.1	50.2	55.2	49.1	51.3	55.0
Texas Average	45.3	46.2	44.9	47.2	45.5	49.1	41.3	43.1	45.6
National Rank	43	44	44	45	46	46	48	48	49

SOURCE: Lester Milbrath, "Participation in the American States," in Herbert Jacob and Kenneth N. Vines, *Politics in the American States,* 2nd ed. (Boston: Little, Brown, 1971), pp. 38–39. For elections 1968–1980, see *Statistical Abstract of the United States,* 1976, 1979, 1983, 1986, and 1989 (Washington, D.C.: U.S. Government Printing Office), pp. 469, 513, 491, 255, and 259, respectively. For 1996, 2000, and 2004 elections, see FEC Web site, Voter Registration and Turnout 1996, 2000, and 2004.

Texas, with Texan George H. Bush on the ballot and with Texan H. Ross Perot running a third-party campaign for the presidency. This factor obviously increased voter turnout in Texas. Even so, Texas still ranked forty-sixth among the fifty states in turnout in 1992 (see Table 3.1). In the 2000 election, with Governor George W. Bush on the ballot for president, the turnout only reached 43.1 percent.

In nonpresidential general elections, for U.S. senators and representatives, held in the years between presidential elections, voter turnout has been even lower. In 1966, Texas had the lowest voter turnout in the nation, with only 20.9 percent of the voting-age population casting ballots. In 1974, Texas was forty-ninth in voter turnout, and in 1982 forty-eighth, with only Georgia and Louisiana ranked lower (see Table 3.2).

Reasons for Low Turnout

Scholars of voting behavior generally fall into two camps. First is the group that believes that socioeconomic characteristics determine who will vote. Results of voting studies generally agree that nonvoters are more often to be found among the poor and undereducated, especially minority-group members. These characteristics are the reasons that this group of people does not vote. In other words, if people were not poor and uneducated, they would vote. Based on this theory and the demographic characteristics of Texas from Chapter 1, it is easy to see why voter turnout in Texas is lower than in states with better family income and education figures.

T A B L E 3.2 Percentage of Voter Turnout in Nonpresidential General Elections 1966–2002

	1966	1970	1974	1978	1982	1986	1990	1994	1998	2002
U.S. Average	45.4	43.5	36.1	35.3	38.0	33.4	33.1	36.0	36.4	36.2
Texas Average	20.9	27.5	18.4	24.1	26.2	25.5	26.8	31.3	26.1	28.8
National Rank	50	47	49	46	48	45	42	45	47	45

SOURCE: FEC Web site http://www.fec.gov Voter Registration and Turnout Statistics.

The second group of scholars believes that the social-psychological model confounds cause with consequences. This group bases its belief on the idea that legal and administrative barriers prevent the poor and uneducated from voting. It is a theory based on two areas of data: first, the cross-national comparison of voting turnout. Only a few nations of the world have higher levels of income and education than the United States, but many more can claim a higher voter turnout. A good example of this is the Mexican presidential election of 1994. Mexico, obviously, has a much lower level of education and income than the United States, but managed an impressive 75 percent turnout of voters in this election. While the honesty in reporting the votes might be in question, the level of turnout was not. Why don't income and education factors affect voting in other nations as they supposedly do in the United States?

Second, the voter turnout in the nineteenth century in the United States was much higher than today, even with the lower levels of education and income at the time. The legal-and-administrative-barrier scholars believe that two major factors have caused lower voting turnouts in Texas and the United States. The first factor is voter registration laws. In spite of all the constitutional amendments, court cases, and voting rights laws, the United States is the only democracy in the world that makes the individual citizen responsible for registering to vote. In other democracies, the government takes responsibility for registering citizens to vote, because voting is considered such an essential activity in a democracy.

A second factor is that political parties have not tried as hard to mobilize poor and less-educated voters as they do wealthier and more-educated voters. It can be argued that the political process in the twenty-first century in the United States has not appealed to the issues in which the poor and less educated are interested. Since the 1980s, the whole political discussion of issues has shifted from what government can do to solve problems to the idea that government itself is the major problem.

This dispute over voter turnout has led to an important discussion about Voting Age Population (VAP) versus Voting Eligible Population (VEP). Voting Eligible Population refers to citizens registered to vote, and will certainly be influenced by state registration laws. Voting Age Population is what percentage of the population is eligible to vote if registered. This distinction is used in Tables 3.1 and 3.2 as a base and to show what impact registration laws may have on voting. Regardless of whether one supports the socioeconomic model or the legal-administrative model, it is clear that voter turnout in Texas is much lower than in other states of the union. Most scholars agree that in a democracy, a low level of participation is not a desirable state of affairs.

Voting Reform

In 1987, the legislature did pass legislation to reform absentee voting in Texas. The law allows voters to vote absentee in person instead of by mail only. In addition, the law dropped the requirement to swear an oath in order to qualify. A final provision allowed absentee votes to be cast in numerous substations in grocery stores and malls in urban counties. Voting substations will usually have punch-card ballots rather than printed ballots in voting machines. In 1989, the legislature extended the absentee-voting period to begin twenty-two days before the election. As a result, absentee voting has increased tremendously. In the 2004 election, more than one-third of the votes for president in Texas were cast before election day.[1] Although absentee votes are not counted until Election Day; early voting does have a major impact on campaign strategy. A last-minute media blitz is not as effective as it was before early voting was established.

Some other obvious steps would improve voter turnout in Texas in particular and the United States in general. The states of Maine, Minnesota, and Wisconsin permit election-day registration of voters, and North Dakota has no voter registration at all. Oregon has mail-in voting available for all voters. It is like voter registration in other nations, where the government takes responsibility for registration. All of these states have among the highest voter turnout figures in the United States. While they also have much smaller populations than Texas, they illustrate what is possible. Other suggested reforms are to hold elections on Sunday, or to declare Election Day a state or national holiday. These changes could increase the number of voters registered, as well as the number of voters, and would help to lessen stress at the polls.

TYPES OF ELECTIONS

Nominations

To begin the election process, political parties must nominate their candidates for public office. Society benefits from the party nominating process, as conflicts between competing factions within the party are resolved. This usually results in a "closing of ranks" as the competing factions unite behind the candidate of the victorious coalition of interests.

Theoretically, nominations by parties also reduce the number of potential candidates for an office, making it easier for the electorate to evaluate the candidates intelligently. Party labels serve as reference points for voters.

History of Nominations   Three methods of nominating candidates have evolved over the years.

The Caucus   The selection of a party's candidate by a very small group of party influentials involves a *nominating caucus,* a common method of nominating candidates early in our nation's history. Several advantages of the caucus are that it is inexpensive, increases party ideological cohesion, and resolves conflict between leaders of party factions because compromises can be more easily reached within a relatively small group.

The advantages of the nominating caucus may also be viewed as disadvantages. The control of the party's nominations by a small group can be seen as undemocratic; as the group usually meets in secret, a basic distrust of the caucus as a nominating process results. Nominating committees of community "good government" organizations rarely use the caucus in Texas, except informally.

The Convention   As a result of Jacksonian democracy, "King Caucus" came under attack and was largely replaced by the nominating convention. This opened the process to more participants and thus increased participation by party activists. There was also greater psychological allegiance to the party by the convention participants. It became easier to receive input from "rank-and-file" party members who identified strongly with the party but who were not "influentials." The convention is also a relatively inexpensive way to nominate candidates. Finally, when used extensively, the nominating convention increases party influence over candidate selection and ideology. The convention system is still used to nominate presidential and vice-presidential candidates.

Primary Elections   The party primary, which gained popularity during the Progressive period early last century, was designed to further democratize the nominating process. Texas first began using the primary with the passage of the Terrell Election Law in 1905. A residual effect of the Terrell Law was that it established the Democratic Party as the preeminent party in the state.

Originally the Terrell Law mandated an *indirect primary,* which required a complex method of nomination, with the delegates to the state convention voting as directed by the primary. By 1918 the *direct primary* was being used and the candidate was nominated directly by the voters. Because a majority was required, a runoff primary was necessary if no candidate received a majority in the first primary. Texas's present primary system retains these characteristics.

The primary has done much to democratize the nominating process. No longer do either high party officials (by caucus) or party activists (by convention) nominate a party's candidate. This enables a potential candidate to create as large a base of support as possible in order to combat the nominee of the other party at the polls. However, the primary is expensive, and candidates must either be wealthy or receive substantial financial support in order to be taken seriously. This may in effect restrict nominating power to a few wealthy or influential persons. Today, an important source of campaign funds comes from political action committees (PACs). (PACs will be discussed in more detail in Chapter 4.)

PARTICIPATION   In the purest sense, a primary is simply the rank-and-file membership of a party choosing a candidate. On this assumption, only party members should vote in that party's primary. But who constitutes a party member? What can people who consider themselves Independents do to determine who will hold most offices, except to vote in a party primary?

In Texas, one result of these problems is "crossover" voting. Many who consider themselves conservatives, whether Democrats, Republicans, or Independents, vote in the first and second Democratic primaries—usually to defeat the liberal candidate. Then, in the general election in November, large numbers of these same "Democrats" tend to vote for Republican nominees—especially those for national or statewide offices. However, liberal Democrats then join the conservative Democrats to defeat the Republicans in the general election. Crossover voting has helped perpetuate conservative Democratic control of state government. This formula for conservative Democratic victory is by no means fool-proof, however, and Republicans are competing more successfully—especially for the offices of high visibility.

In order for a candidate to win a primary election, he or she must receive a majority of the votes cast. If no one candidate has a majority, then a runoff election must be held between the two top vote getters in the primary.

RESTRICTIONS   Because primaries are considered elections, some states have developed methods to ensure that only party members vote in primaries. The *closed primary* is one such method. Potential voters must register as members of a specific party or as independents. They are then allowed to vote only in their designated party's primary. If they consider themselves independents, they cannot vote in any party's primary. Voters usually must register at least thirty days prior to a primary. The *open primary* allows any registered voter to vote in the primary of any party, but he or she may vote in only one party's primary.

The Texas system is essentially a mixture of the two. Voters are not required to register as members of a party in order to vote in primary elections. But if they vote in the primary or participate in a convention of any party, at that point they become members of that party. The system then becomes closed for future party activity in that year. For example, a voter who votes in the Republican primary is considered a Republican for that election year and cannot participate in either the precinct convention or second primary (runoff) of another party. The establishment of party membership does not, of course, prevent the voter from voting for the candidates of any party in the general election.

PRESIDENTIAL PRIMARIES   In Texas, the candidates of a party are nominated directly by the primary voters—thus the term *direct primary.* When presidential primaries are held in some states, however, the nomination is indirect. That is, the primary voters elect delegates to the party convention, who in turn nominate the party's presidential and vice-presidential candidates. The formula used to determine the number of delegates won by each nominee and their degree of commitment at the convention is established by each state and varies accordingly.

In 1976, Texas experimented with its first presidential primary. Critics charged that the primary was a subterfuge developed by the Democratic Texas legislature to push all of Texas's delegate support for president at the national convention to Lloyd Bentsen, then Texas's Democratic junior senator. It was feared that his support would be split if the usual convention method for selecting delegates were used. Texas's first presidential primary law was designed to self-destruct following that one election, which further prompted cynics to dub the law "the Bentsen primary." The voters, however, made the "Bentsen primary" a "Carter and Reagan primary," as Ronald Reagan won all the delegates to the Republican convention and Jimmy Carter won an overwhelming majority of delegates to the Democratic convention.

In 1988, Texas created a presidential primary that was a mixture of direct and indirect primaries. Some delegates representing a presidential candidate were selected as a result of the primary vote (a direct primary). Other delegates were selected by the political party convention process (an indirect primary). (See Chapter 4 for further discussion.)

The presidential primary in Texas is conducted on the second Tuesday in March of even-numbered years. It is nicknamed "Super Tuesday" because many other southern states hold their primaries on that day, deciding a large number of convention delegates. The basic idea was to create primaries early in the presidential campaign, which would tend to favor a more conservative presidential candidate. This was supposed to help southern conservative Democrats running for president. In 1988, however, liberal candidate Michael Dukakis did well on Super Tuesday and won the Democratic Party presidential nomination.

In 1986, the Texas legislature rescheduled the primary to nominate all state officials on the second Tuesday in March in both presidential and nonpresidential election years. In 1992, at the Southern Regional Primary, moderate Democrat Bill Clinton did well in the primary and won the Democratic Party presidential nomination, and was elected president. This change to an earlier date for presidential primaries is called "frontloading," and is an attempt by a state to increase its influence in national politics. (See a sample primary election ballot in Figure 3.2.)

General Elections

General elections are held to allow voters to choose, from competing political party nominees who have won their primary and from write-in candidates, who will hold national, state, and county offices. In order for a candidate to win office, he or she must obtain only a plurality vote. (The winning candidate must receive at least one vote more than any other opponent.)

General elections are held in Texas on the first Tuesday after the first Monday in November of even-numbered years. This is the date established for national elections for president, vice president, U.S. senators, and representatives. Almost all states also hold all their state elections on this same day.

In presidential election years, the voter turnout is traditionally at its highest. In "off-year" elections, between presidential elections, the turnout is less, and Texans elect the governor and most other state officials. Elections are set up this way so that conservative-moderate state officials are not burdened by having to share the ballot with a liberal-moderate Democratic presidential nominee. There are usually a large number of proposed amendments to the Texas Constitution on any general election ballot.

Special Elections

Special elections are held to meet special or emergency needs such as a constitutional amendment or to fill vacancies in public offices caused by death, resignation, or impeachment. This type of election is nonpartisan, and thus avoids the need for a primary. While the candidate's political party is not listed on the ballot,

B **C**

(Condado de)
HOUSTON COUNTY, TEXAS

MARCH 14, 2000

(14 de marzo de 2000)

INSTRUCTION NOTE:
Vote for the candidate of your choice in each race by darkening in the oval provided to the left of the name of the candidate. You may vote for a write-in candidate by writing in the name of the candidate on the line provided and darkening in the oval provided to the left of the line. You may vote for one presidential candidate whose name appears on the ballot by darkening in the oval provided to the left of the name of the candidate or you may vote as uncommitted by darkening the oval provided to the left of "Uncommitted." Make only one choice.
"I am a Republican and understand that I am ineligible to vote or participate in another political party's primary election or convention during this voting year."
Use only the marker provided.
(NOTA DE INSTRUCCION:
Vote por el candidato de su preferencia en cada carrera llenando completamente el espacio ovalado a la izquierda del nombre del candidato. Usted podrá votar por inserción escrita escribiendo el nombre del candidato en la línea provista y llenando completamente el espacio ovalado a la izquierda de la línea. Usted puede votar por un candidato para presidente cuyo nombre aparece en la boleta por llenando completamente el espacio ovalado a la izquierda del nombre del candidato o usted puede votar como votante no comprometido por llenando completamente el espacio ovalado a la izquierda de las palabras no comprometido. Haga solamente una selección.
"Yo soy Republicano y comprendo que no estoy elegible para votar o participar en la elección primaria o la convención de algún otro partido político durante este año electoral."
Solamente use el marcador provisto.)

Preference for Presidential Nominee
(Preferencia para un Candidato Nombrado para Presidente)

( ) Alan Keyes

( ) John McCain

( ) Gary Bauer

( ) Charles Bass Urban

( ) Orrin G. Hatch

( ) Steve Forbes

( ) George W. Bush

( ) Uncommitted

United States Senator
(Senador de los Estados Unidos)
( ) Kay Bailey Hutchison

Railroad Commissioner
(Comisionado de Ferrocarriles)
( ) Charles R. Matthews

Railroad Commissioner, Unexpired Term
(Comisionado de Ferrocarriles, Duración Restante del Cargo)
( ) Michael L. Williams

( ) Andy Draughn

Justice, Supreme Court, Place 1
(Juez, Corte Suprema, Lugar Núm. 1)
( ) Valorie W. Davenport

( ) Nathan Hecht

Justice, Supreme Court, Place 2
(Juez, Corte Suprema, Lugar Núm. 2)
( ) Priscilla Owen

Justice, Supreme Court, Place 3
(Juez, Corte Suprema, Lugar Núm. 3)
( ) Rod E. Gorman

( ) Al Gonzales

Presiding Judge, Court of Criminal Appeals
(Juez Presidente, Corte de Apelaciones Criminales)

( ) Connie J. Kelley

( ) J. Gary Trichter

( ) Tom Price

( ) Sharon Keller

Judge, Court of Criminal Appeals, Place 1
(Juez, Corte de Apelaciones Criminales, Lugar Núm. 1)

( ) Charles Holcomb

( ) Alan Curry

( ) Tom Greenwell

( ) John Boston

( ) Guy Williams

Judge, Court of Criminal Appeals, Place 2
(Juez, Corte de Apelaciones Criminales, Lugar Núm. 2)

( ) W.B. "Bennie" House

( ) Jim Wallace

( ) Barbara Parker Hervey

( ) Sally L. Ray

( ) Pat Barber

Justice, 12th Court of Appeals District
(Juez, Corte de Apelaciones, Distrito 12)

( ) Sam Griffith

( ) Roby Hadden

Sheriff
(Sherife)
( ) Darrel E. Bobbitt

County Commissioner, Precinct No. 1
(Comisionado del Condado, Precinto Núm. 1)

( ) Weldon Bailey

( ) Joe Daniels

Constable, Precinct No. 2
(Condestable, Precinto Núm. 2)
( ) Kenneth (Red) Smith

County Chairman
(Presidente del Condado)
( ) Joni K. McCreight

( ) _____
Write-in *(Voto Escrito)*

INSTRUCTION NOTE:
Darken in the oval provided to the left of the statement indicating the way you desire to vote.
Use only the marker provided.
(NOTA DE INSTRUCCION:
Llene completamente el espacio ovalado a la izquierda de la frase que indica la manera en que quiere votar.
Solamente use el marcador provisto.)

Proposition No. 1
(Proposición Núm. 1)

"Shall student initiated prayer be allowed at school sporting events?"
("¿Deberá ser permitido oraciones religiosas iniciadas por parte de los estudiantes durante eventos deportivos escolares?")

( ) Yes *(Si)*

( ) No *(No)*

01-01F   **B**   **C**

FIGURE 3.2 Sample Primary Ballot

51

voters are usually made well aware of a candidate's political persuasion. Since 1961, in Texas, special elections have required a majority vote to win. So, similar to a primary election, a runoff election between the two top vote getters may be necessary to determine who will win the office in a special election.

In 1993, a special election was held to fill the U.S. Senate seat vacated by Lloyd Bentsen, who had become Secretary of the Treasury in the Clinton administration. No candidate received a majority of the votes. In a runoff, Republican Kay Bailey Hutchison defeated Robert Krueger, who had been appointed to the Senate seat by former Governor Ann Richards.

City and Special District Elections

Because of reforms from the Progressive Era, elections to fill the offices for cities or special districts are held on a regular basis to fill specified terms of office. These elections are usually nonpartisan. Although political parties or organizations of "concerned citizens" that perform all the functions of a party may support candidates, no label on the ballot informs the voter of that support. In fact, this is the basic purpose of the nonpartisan election—to force the voter to select "the person, not the party." Usually, these organizations of citizens do not mobilize as many voters as political parties do, so voter turnout in nonpartisan elections is usually lower than turnout in partisan elections.

CONCLUSION

Political participation in Texas has been characterized by a long history of both formal and informal restraints. Election law and registration procedures have kept many otherwise eligible citizens from voting. The Texas political culture has provided an environment in which voting was not given a very high priority, especially among minority populations. As a result, Texas has had among the lowest voter turnout, when compared with the other forty-nine states.

Scholars usually attribute lower voter turnout to socioeconomic characteristics or legal and administrative barriers. Texas, with its low family income and education figures, and long history of legal barriers to voting, can readily fit either model.

Some states, such as Maine, Minnesota, and Wisconsin, have reformed registration procedures to permit election-day registration of voters. This has led to a higher voter turnout in those states. Similar election reforms in Texas would probably increase voter turnout there.

Although voters can be confused by the number of elections, beginning with the primary and possible runoff election in the spring, the general election in the fall, and possible special elections at other times, it is important that citizens take a more active role in the election process. The disputed nature of the 2000 presidential election, with George Bush winning the presidency without winning a majority of the popular vote, underlines the importance of voter awareness and participation.

In the next chapter, we will examine the role that interest groups and political parties play in the election process.

KEY TERMS

caucus	nonpartisan election	special election
convention	office-block ballot	Voting Rights Act
"frontloading"	party-column ballot	white primary
general election	primary election	

Logging On

The expansion of voting rights in the United States and Texas has been greatly influenced by constitutional amendments to the U.S. Constitution since the Civil War. Look at the 15th, 17th, 19th, 23rd, 24th, and 26th Amendments at **http://www.law.cornell.edu/ constitution/constitution.table.html#amendments**.

To look at the latest election information and early voting and voter registration laws, go to the Texas Secretary of State election page at **http:// www.sos.state.tx.us**.

ENDNOTES

1. Election Reform Information Project, electionline.org.

4

Interest Groups, Political Parties, and Campaigning

INTRODUCTION

During each biennial legislative session, the halls of the stately old pink granite capitol in Austin are crowded daily with various groups of people who all have something in common: They want something from their government. These Texans come from all walks of life, and are concerned about a wide range of problems. Some may be farmers worried about the rising cost of electricity needed to run irrigation pumps; a few may be doctors faced with staggering increases in malpractice insurance premiums; others may be businessmen wanting to be freed from what they feel is excessive government regulation.

Public school teachers seeking a pay raise and an equalization of school funding try to convince legislators that their cause is worthy of a higher priority than other state funding needs. Others, though, may be concerned about problems for which state government can offer little help. Farmers concerned about declining farm income and the decreasing number of family farming operations may get a sympathetic hearing in Austin, but the problem is national in scope, and any meaningful action will have to come from the federal government. Some people may be in Austin only because others, interested in the same problems but having different viewpoints, have preceded them. For example, finance industry representatives who seek to persuade the state government to allow higher interest rates may find that leaders for consumer groups have already made known their opposition to such a move.

Political parties also play a part in the process of individuals seeking, through interest groups, to influence government decisions. Parties recruit attractive candidates to seek public office. These candidates will appeal to interest groups, in order to build a winning coalition. Parties will use their organizational structure to mobilize voters, and to assist the candidate in campaigning to win public office. Once elected to office, party members will attempt to work together to satisfy the interests of their winning coalition.

The relationship between interest groups and political parties has changed in recent years. Parties have weakened because of declining public support and reforms that have diminished the role of party leaders. In contrast, interest groups have increased in number, and their role in campaigns has enlarged because of the Federal Election Campaign Act amendments of 1974.[1] Interest groups have created political action committees (PACs), which have become a major source of campaign funds.

INFORMAL AND FORMAL INTEREST GROUPS

Nearly everyone in Texas is interested to some degree in the policies and actions of state government. Thus, most Texans, whether they realize it or not, are associated with one or more *interest groups*. These groups may have no formal organization but consist of people concerned about governmental actions and regulations that affect them. In any legislative session, bills dealing with hundreds of different topics are considered, and many whose interests may be affected follow their progress. A bill revamping our property tax system would affect all homeowners, business property owners, real estate persons, investors, and public school officials. Bills dealing with the oil industry would be of interest to workers and managers in that industry, as well as to those who own oil company stocks. Students may not become too excited about property tax or oil industry bills, but legislation dealing with tuition increases or student government could easily fill an auditorium with people sharing similar interests.

It is difficult to imagine any Texan whose daily activities are not affected in some way by state government decisions. Texans with similar interests may show their concern in varying degrees. Proposed changes at any level of governmental policy making may cause a few hundred interested parties to travel to Austin. Others with similar interests may try to communicate directly with their governmental representative, while still others may be content to simply follow the controversy in the newspapers.

When an interest group becomes formally organized, it often becomes what is commonly known as a *pressure group.* When people with similar interests form an organization or association for the purpose of accomplishing stated objectives and influencing elected and appointed officials, they have formed a pressure group. Some pressure groups in Texas have large and dedicated memberships, politically knowledgeable leaders, and financial resources sufficient to maintain permanent headquarters and staff in Austin to handle matters affecting their members. Other pressure groups, with fewer members and resources, may not have a full-time staff in Austin but may occasionally either send a representative or hire one of Austin's many law firms or freelance *lobbyists* to represent them. Other groups occasionally spring up around highly visible issues and sometimes attain tremendous though short-lived influence. The successful pressure group is concerned with influencing governmental policy in several areas.

1. Legislative—Attention must be paid to supporting desired legislation, opposing undesired legislation, and gaining sufficient state funding for desired programs already in existence.
2. Judicial—Judicial decisions following the passage of major legislation often determine how legislation will be interpreted for years to come, and interest groups must be sure that their views are considered before decisions are made. They must also pay attention to other legal battles involving interests of the group.
3. Executive—Groups must follow closely the decisions of state agencies working in areas of concern to the group; testimony explaining why the group wants certain actions may be presented.
4. Constitutional—At times, certain interest groups must work toward changes in the state constitution that favor their members' interests.
5. Public Opinion—Groups can develop advertising campaigns that are designed to influence the public's attitude toward the group—for example, the "Eat Beef" campaign of the Cattle Raisers' Association.

Making governmental laws and regulations involves compromise among the various groups concerned. Those who make these laws and regulations, usually legislators and executive officials, must consider the requests and needs of all the concerned parties and then somehow arrive at a compromise position that expresses the *public interest*—that is, the desire of the people for laws that preserve and protect the interests of society as a whole. For example, the finance industry desires high interest rates that allow maximum profits for lenders. Consumer groups, on the other hand, prefer low interest rates that make loans cheap and available to all. The public interest, however, is best served by interest rates somewhere in between: high enough to encourage lenders to make loans available for new homes, cars, and other goods, yet low enough to make credit available to those who meet reasonable qualifications.

INTERESTS IN TEXAS

Texas's tremendous size and widely differing regions make for an unusually large variety of political interests. The Texas legislature, in the view of some observers, is the most divergent of any state legislature in the country. This variety of interests, beliefs, and philosophies has led to much organization, both formal and informal, of interest and pressure groups. The most significant of these groups promote the interests of business and industry, labor, agriculture, the various professions, veterans, consumers, and religious and ethnic groups. Many of the most influential interest and pressure groups in Texas have banded together because of common economic interests.

Business

Business leaders and business-related organizations wield considerable influence in Texas for a number of reasons. For one thing, rapid economic development is still a fact of life in Texas, and many, both in and out of the business world, consider a "healthy business climate" a legitimate social goal. Business leaders also tend to appreciate the need for organization, research, and careful planning—traits that lead to success in the political world as often as they do in the business world. Business representatives can usually count on a sympathetic hearing from state government, because a good many legislators and appointed board and commission members come from the ranks of business.

Business is usually thought of as a conservative political force in Texas. The business community can generally be counted on to defend and protect the established political, economic, and social structures. Business groups constantly lobby governmental decision makers, seeking such benefits as better transportation and marketing facilities, protection from excessive competition, limits on the rights of employees and customers, subsidies, and tax breaks. Leaders of the business community talk gushingly about laissez-faire and the free-market economy, but they often are the first in line when government subsidies, tax breaks, and the like are passed out. Certain outspoken businesspersons may grumble occasionally about excessive government interference, but some kinds of government regulation have been welcomed by business for years. Especially appreciated have been government regulations designed to limit competition or to stipulate price floors on certain commodities. In Texas, the infant oil industry led the fight in the 1930s to give the Texas Railroad Commission power to set production levels for oil wells.

One of the more prominent business groups in Texas is the Texas Association of Business (TAB), formerly the Texas Manufacturers' Association. TAB lobbyists have played an influential role on the state political scene for years, looking out mainly for the interests of large corporations and business firms with respect to such matters as labor relations, taxation, economic development, and product liability legislation. Another well-known group, the Texas Research League (TRL), describes itself as "a nonprofit corporation" engaged in objective analyses of the operation, programs, and problems of Texas government. The TRL is financed largely by contributions from business and corporate interests, and its board of directors is truly a blue-chip listing of the most powerful and influential leaders of the Texas business community. Since its inception in 1952, the TRL has produced hundreds of reports on various aspects of state government, studies that have often been the foundation for legislative and administrative policy decisions. Most state officials have nothing but high praise for the TRL's work; and the group's studies consistently win major national research awards. Occasional criticism comes from Texas liberals, who claim that the League's information reflects a probusiness or prowealth slant.

In addition to these broad-based business groups, literally dozens of more specialized trade associations look after the interests of various segments of the business community. Among the more active of these trade associations are groups promoting the interests of Texas real estate persons, automobile dealers, bankers, savings and loan associations, small loan firms, brewers, builders, contractors, apartment owners, railroads, petroleum industry firms, and nursing homes.

Professions

Professional lobbyists and interest groups have increased their political skills and clout in recent years. At one time, medicine, law, teaching, and the clergy would have been considered the only professions, but many other occupational groups, seeing the advantages of professional licensing and regulatory organizations, have persuaded the legislature to grant them professional status. The state now exercises some form of control over accountants, nurses, architects, barbers, cosmetologists, surveyors, engineers, pharmacists, morticians, and real estate persons. Some of these professional groups have become politically influential; the Texas Trial Lawyers' Association and the Texas State Teachers' Association, for example, are among the most powerful lobbies in the state.

State regulation of these professions probably has benefited most Texans. Some regulatory boards have been criticized, however, for growing too close to the professions being regulated. According to their critics, the regulatory boards have been more concerned with preserving the incomes and status of the profession than with serving the interests of the public.

Agriculture

Texas was first of all a farming and ranching society, and agricultural groups have had at least some degree of influence in Austin for over a century. The best-known farm group today is the Texas Farm Bureau Federation, which usually reflects the desires of the "agribusiness" community. Another group, the Texas

Farmers' Union, developed in response to the problems of small-scale agriculture during the 1930s. Also active are the Texas and Southwestern Cattle Raisers' Association, which represents the interests of cattle ranchers, and the Texas Sheep and Goat Raisers' Association.

Labor Unions

In a few areas of Texas, labor unions wield some political influence. The labor vote is probably most important in Houston and other cities (Beaumont, Port Arthur, and Galveston) in heavily unionized areas along the Texas Gulf Coast. On the statewide level, organized labor has not been too important a political force. The Texas AFL-CIO, which includes many but not all of the state's most important unions, can turn out workers and contributions, but its membership is concentrated in certain areas, and many legislators are relatively unaffected by its activities. Labor's goals sometimes coincide with those of other business groups; when this happens, labor wins a few legislative battles. When other major interests oppose Texas labor, however, it usually does not prevail.

Due to an increasing area of employment in the state economy in government, public employee unions have become important. A good example of this type of group is the American Federation of State, County, and Municipal Employees (AFSCME). These groups of public employees have collective bargaining rights, but they do not have the right to strike.

Ethnic Groups

Ethnic political organizations have gained importance in recent years. Probably the most influential African American group is the National Association for the Advancement of Colored People (NAACP), which has used the judicial process to win impressive victories in the areas of voting rights, equal educational opportunities, and redistricting of county precinct lines. Mexican American political groups began forming over fifty years ago, but these groups had little impact until after World War II. These groups include the League of United Latin American Citizens (LULAC), the American G.I. Forum, and the Mexican American Legal Defense Fund (MALDEF). With the use of lawsuits, MALDEF has been very significant in efforts to bring about equal educational funding for both K–12 public education and higher education in South Texas.

Probably the key to political influence for ethnic groups in Texas is voter registration and turnout. Typically, African American and Mexican American precincts have a much lower percentage of registered voters than do the more affluent Anglo precincts, and the actual voter turnout on Election Day is usually lower in minority areas.

Other Interests

Several other types of interest groups have been active in Texas in recent years. Single-interest groups have become more important in the political process in general. These groups do not care about broad policy areas, but instead try to force officials to take a stand on a single issue. A good example of this type of group is the National Rifle Association (NRA). This group's single issue is to focus on any legislation that limits the ownership and use of guns. In 1994 this group, against overwhelming public support, was almost able to defeat a national crime bill because one provision contained a ban on assault rifles.

Public-interest groups have sprung up since the 1970s. These groups try to look at public-policy issues from the standpoint of what is best for the average citizen. An example of this type of group is Common Cause, which is concerned with the elimination of corruption and conflicts of interest in government. This group, of course, has been active in Texas.

Religious groups have taken an interest in politics, particularly since the U.S. Supreme Court case *Roe v. Wade* (1973), which overturned a law prohibiting abortion. The Catholic Church has become very active in groups such as the right-to-life advocates in Houston and the Texas Right-to-Life Organization. The Texas Abortion Rights Action League was formed to support the *Roe v. Wade* decision.

Protestant religious groups have also been active. One of the best known is the Christian Life Commission of the Baptist General Convention of Texas, which has fought a losing battle against the state lottery, but continues to fight against casino gambling. Fundamentalist Protestant groups have been very active in the Republican Party and in local school board elections. Prayer in school and a traditional school curriculum are key issues.

Finally, environmental interest groups made a big impact in Texas in the 1990s. A good example of this type of group is the Sierra Club. This organization was responsible for several lawsuits that dealt with the problem of development threatening the habitat of endangered wildlife, both flora and fauna. They also were responsible for putting such issues as the conservation of our water supply in various aquifers on the public agenda. The Bush administration, since 2001, has generally taken environmental issues off the public agenda.

LOBBYING

The policy decisions made by state and local governments in Texas can have a tremendous impact on the interest and pressure groups just mentioned. Almost all of these groups, along with others not mentioned, actively try to influence such decisions. This attempt to influence the governmental decision-making process is called *lobbying,* and the agents who do this are *lobbyists.* The techniques that a group chooses are usually based on the monetary resources available. To hire a lobbyist can be very expensive.

Lobbyists use a number of different methods to influence government policy making. Perhaps the most widely known method is direct contact with legislators. This can include personal visits, distributing informational pamphlets concerning the lobby group's views, presenting witnesses to testify on the lobby group's position at legislative hearings and meetings, and mingling with legislators at the many social functions held in conjunction with legislative sessions.

Many people believe that this "social lobbying" is the lobbyist's most important work. Each legislative session usually produces a large number of newspaper accounts of free drinks, free food, and free parties. There is indeed a great deal of this social lobbying, and members of the legislature are deluged with invitations to all manner of receptions, luncheons, and parties. Legislators could probably live almost entirely on free food and drink during the days they stay in Austin. "If you accepted every drink forced on you and ate everything available," said one lawmaker to a reporter, "you'd wind up a 300-pound alcoholic." Yet, in spite of this widespread social lobbying, most political observers downplay its influence on the legislative decision-making process. Other lobbying tools, according to many legislators and professional lobbyists, are far more important in determining how successful a lobbyist will be in influencing legislation.

These other tools include organizing members of the lobbyist's interest group to generate letters and phone calls about key legislation, recruiting and financing legislative candidates likely to be sympathetic to the interest group's goals, and promoting a friendly public attitude toward the overall goals of the interest group. Shortly before the 1979 legislative session, for example, savings and loan association lobbyists, who supported a bill raising the legal ceiling on mortgage interest rates from 10 percent to 12 percent, traveled all over the state presenting their case to newspaper editorial boards.

The best lobbyists are often former members of the legislature, who usually have a better-than-usual grasp of the intricacies of the entire political process. The contacts these former legislators developed during their legislative service are most useful to them as lobbyists. In recent years, many influential legislative staffers have also become lobbyists. In 1991, Ben Barnes, a former lieutenant governor and speaker of the house, and former speaker Bill Clayton were registered as lobbyists. (See Table 4.1 for groups with the most lobbyists.)

Executive and Judicial Lobbying

Interest groups maintain a watchful eye not only on the legislature, but also on decision making in the executive and judicial branches. After all, once the legislators have made the law, it is up to the administrators to enforce it and the judges to interpret it. A ruling from a bureaucrat or judge could abruptly negate a masterful job of influencing the legislative process toward a certain policy decision. Similarly, a favorable ruling could counter the effect of a law considered unfavorable by a particular interest group. Lobbying bureaucrats is much like lobbying legislators: direct contact, distribution of research information, and presentation of witnesses before administrative hearings are all important tasks. It is also helpful to ensure that people with attitudes favorable to an interest group are appointed to positions on the various boards and commissions. Many interest groups try to play an active role in this appointment process by recommending names to the governor when vacancies occur.

Interest groups occasionally try to influence the judicial branch of government, though this attempt is used only when legislative lobbying and executive lobbying have proved unsuccessful. This type of lobbying sometimes takes the form of

T A B L E 4.1 Number of Lobbyists Reporting By Interest Represented, 2002

Interest Represented	Number of Lobbyists
Business and Commerce	1333
Corporations and Associations	1025
City Government	796
Taxation	794
Civil Remedies	749
State Agencies, Boards, and Commissions	747
Consumer Protection	731
County Government	706
Insurance	647
Health and Health Care	646
Environment	641
Economic and Industrial Development	638
Tort Reform	608
State Finance	604
Utilities	597

SOURCE: State Ethics Commission, 2002, *Lobbyists Subject Matter Categories*. Retrieved December 27, 2002, from www.ethics.state.tx.us/tedd/lobsub2002a.html. Printed in Maxwell and Crain, *Texas Politics Today*, 11 ed., p. 145.

"friend-of-the-court" briefs filed in major lawsuits involving members of the interest group. Ethnic groups and environmental groups have been successful in this area.

REGULATING INTEREST GROUPS AND LOBBYISTS

Any set of laws regulating the activities of interest groups and lobbyists should prevent corrupt influence-peddling practices such as bribery without discouraging political participation on the part of the average citizen. The right to petition one's government is basic to our system, and neither the highly paid professional lobbyist nor the average citizen should feel intimidated by laws regulating the way in which he or she petitions the government. Finding proper regulation has proven to be difficult not only in Texas, but in other states.

Following the Sharpstown Bank scandal in the early 1970s, which involved illegal payments to members of the legislature including the speaker of the house, the 63rd Legislature in 1973 enacted a lobby regulation reform law. This law requires persons who communicate directly with a member or employee of the legislative or executive branch to register as lobbyists if they either (1) spend $200 per quarter (except for their own food, lodging, and travel), or (2) lobby for someone else for compensation or as a part of their regular employment duties.

The registrants are required to file monthly expense reports during legislative sessions and quarterly reports between sessions. Contributors of more than $500 to lobby groups must be identified in the reports.

This law has shed some light on the amount of money spent to influence government, but a lack of enforcement and uneven policies concerning what spending should be reported have prevented it from being as effective as its sponsors had hoped.

In 1974, Congress passed the Federal Election Campaign Spending Act, with amendments. This law set up the Federal Election Commission to enforce the provision of campaign financing reform. One of the reforms was a limit on campaign contributions by individuals. This limit led to the tremendous growth of political action committees (PACs), which were created under state and federal laws to allow contributions over the individual limits. Whereas federal law sets limits on PACs, Texas law sets no limits on the amount of money a PAC can give to candidates. In 1976, only 491 PACs were registered in Texas. Today, Texas has the largest number of PACs in the nation, with more than 1,800. PACs are the major source of campaign financing for most incumbent officeholders. In 1990, incumbent members of the Texas Senate collected $1.1 million from PACs. At the same time, 36 house committee chairs received $1.3 million from business-oriented PACs.[2]

In 2002, Congress passed the Bipartisan Campaign Reform Act (BRAC). This law was designed to restrict the amount of "soft money" in political campaigns. However, it provided a number of loopholes. In the 2004 presidential campaign, "527 organizations" became a major campaign issue. 527 organizations are groups not officially connected with a campaign. These groups can spend money to provide information to the public usually unfavorable to one of the candidates. These changes in the law allowed both Bush and Kerry to spend over $200 million each in the 2004 presidential campaign.[3]

POLITICAL PARTIES

Although the Founding Fathers disapproved of political parties, it soon became evident that such organizations would be necessary to conduct the affairs of government. In fact, if we did not have political parties, we would need to invent other institutions to perform the same functions.

Purpose and Functions

The political party is usually a coalition of political, economic, and moral factions that are attempting to gain control of the government in order to further their interests. Political parties perform four significant functions in our political process.

First, political parties nominate and elect their members to public office. This is one of the clear ways to distinguish interest groups from political parties. A second function is for political parties to develop issues or a philosophy (such as liberal or conservative) that is the basis for their campaign. The issues or philosophy provide cues that help voters to choose between the candidates. The third function is to mobilize voters by encouraging participation in the election process. Finally, the fourth function of parties is to run the government, from the courthouse to the White House. The losing party also has a role in government. It becomes the "loyal opposition" party, which acts as a check on the party in power. Let us take a brief look at political party activity in Texas.

The Democrats

The Democratic Party comprises two major factions: the liberals and the conservatives. Although it is easy to overgeneralize, labor unions, small farmers, ranchers, laborers, intellectuals, African Americans, and Mexican Americans usually support the liberal faction. In order to be elected, a liberal candidate must build a coalition consisting of these divergent groups. If he or she attempts to appeal too strongly to one group, there is danger of alienating the others; a successful coalition is fragile at best.

The conservative faction is also split, but its elements are more cohesive than are the liberal ones, though the small-town, agricultural, and small-business conservatives occasionally come into conflict with the Establishment—the large law firms, financial institutions, and large-business and agribusiness interests. The losing faction in the first primary rarely hesitates to support the other conservative candidate if a runoff is necessary.

The conservative-Democratic faction has been more influential in state government than either the liberals in the Democratic Party or the Republicans. Although liberals have almost always lost, until recently there usually was strong factional competition in the primaries. When the liberals have competed successfully for major statewide elective office, such as winning governor, attorney general, comptroller, and land commissioner positions in 1990, this trend has made the Republican Party more competitive as conservative Democrats increasingly join the Republican Party.

The Republicans

The Republican Party in Texas traditionally has appealed to the middle- to upper-income families in urban and suburban communities, especially around Houston and Dallas. Traditionally, German Americans in the Hill Country of Texas, white-collar managerial professionals, and immigrants from the Northeast and Midwest parts of the United States have been Republicans. The results of the last two presidential elections have shown that rural counties have also become strongly Republican.

Party Competition

For a number of years after the Civil War, Texas was a one-party Democratic state. Because the Republican Party was identified with the abuses of power under Reconstruction, almost no Republican candidates were elected in Texas.

In the presidential elections between the Civil War and the 1970s, Texas only voted for the Republican candidates in 1928, 1952, and 1956—primarily because the Democratic presidential candidates were considered too liberal.

In the 1932 presidential election, Texas was part of what was referred to as a realigning election.[4] This concept is an election in which major groups in the electorate shift their political party affiliations. The 1932 election created the "solid South," in which the Democratic Party swept to a massive victory up and down the ballot.

The more recent move toward two-party competition began in 1961. In that year, John Tower, a Republican, was elected to the U.S. Senate, the first Republican senator for Texas since Reconstruction. In spite of this breakthrough, however, there was only one Republican elected to the Texas legislature out of 181 positions.

At the national level, the passage of civil rights legislation by the Democrats under President Lyndon Johnson in the 1960s began to push conservative Democrats toward the Republican Party, especially in presidential voting. This trend in "presidential Republicans"—voters who voted for conservative Democrats at state and local offices, and Republicans for president—was shown in the presidential elections of 1972–1992. The Republican candidate carried Texas in every election with the exception of 1976. That same year, respected conservative Democrat John Connally joined the Republican Party. In 1978, the Republican Party began to have success at the state level in Texas. Republican Bill Clements was elected in 1978 and reelected in 1986, the first Republican elected governor since E. J. Davis in 1870. In 1984, conservative Democrat-turned-Republican Phil Gramm successfully retained John Tower's senate seat for the Republicans.

In the early 1990s, Republican successes continued, as the party captured the state treasurer and agriculture commissioner positions, and elected four members to the Texas Supreme Court. In the Texas legislature, Republican representation in 1991 increased to 66 members out of 181 members of the house and senate. In a special election in 1993, Kay Bailey Hutchison captured the second U.S. Senate seat, giving the Republicans both U.S. Senate seats from Texas.

Republican Dominance

In 1994, the Texas election was submerged in a Republican tidal wave that swept Democrats out of office from coast to coast in the United States. At the national level, Republicans gained control of both houses of Congress for the first time since 1954 and won a majority (30) of governorships for the first time since 1970. In Texas, George W. Bush, the former president's eldest son, won the governorship by beating Democratic incumbent Ann Richards. Republican candidates captured two seats on the Texas Railroad Commission, giving them all three seats. Republican Agriculture Commissioner Rick Perry was reelected, and Republicans gained control of the Texas Supreme Court for the first time since the 1870s. Republican candidates also gained control of the fifteen-member State Board of Education.[5]

Heavily DEMOCRATIC (91 or more Dem points):	*none.*
Strongly DEMOCRATIC (81 to 90 Dem points):	New Jersey (87); Washington (87); Wisconsin (84); Michigan (82).
Mostly DEMOCRATIC (71 to 80 Dem points):	Delaware (79); Massachusetts (78); Hawaii (75); Maryland (72); Oregon (72); Illinois (71); West Virginia (71).
Somewhat DEMOCRATIC (61 to 70 Dem points):	New Mexico (70); California (68); New York (68); Connecticut (66); Iowa (66); Louisiana (66); Rhode Island (61).
Leaning DEMOCRATIC 51 to 60 Dem points):	Maine (60); Vermont (56)[1]; Arkansas (53); Pennsylvania (53); North Carolina (51).
Leaning REPUBLICAN (51 to 60 GOP points):	*Minnesota (51); North Dakota (54); Indiana (53).*
Somewhat REPUBLICAN (61 to 70 GOP points):	*Florida (61); South Dakota (64); Tennessee (64); Oklahoma (67); Missouri (68); Virginia (69); Georgia (70).*
Mostly REPUBLICAN (71 to 80 GOP points):	*Arizona (71); Kansas (72); Nevada (73); South Carolina (73); Wyoming (75); Montana (76).*
Strongly REPUBLICAN (81 to 90 GOP points):	*Nebraska (81)[2]; Mississippi (83); Alabama (84); Texas (87); Colorado (88); Kentucky (88); Ohio (90).*
Heavily REPUBLICAN (91 or more GOP Points):	*Utah (92); Alaska (93); New Hampshire (95); Idaho (96).*

F I G U R E 4.1 Party Competition in the States, 2004
SOURCE: The Green Papers http://www.TheGreenPapers.com.

The Republican victory was not confined just to the national and state level, but was also felt at the local level. In the Texas legislature, Republican representation rose to 61 members in the house and 14 members in the senate. Republicans captured the county government in the traditionally Democratic stronghold of Bexar County (San Antonio), and were elected in several counties in South Texas for the first time in history.[6]

It appears in 1994 that Texas joined the ranks of two-party states. Gary Bruner, executive director of the Republican party in Texas, was so excited about the Republican victories that he believed that Texas was going straight to a modified one-party Republican state without a two-party competition stage.[7] The 1998 election proved Bruner to be a prophet, as Governor George W. Bush won reelection for another four-year term and led the Republican party to sweep all statewide offices, and all seats on the Texas Supreme Court. The 2002 election confirmed this analysis with the Republican Party adding control of both houses of the state legislature. In 2004, after a bitter redistricting battle, Republicans achieved a majority in the U.S. House of Representatives seats in Texas 21 to 11. See Figure 4.1 describing Texas as strongly Republican.

The election of 1994 seems to fit the definition of a *realigning election*. Usually, realignment occurs in a single election, as in the New Deal coalition that brought the Democrats to power in 1932. however, it appears that this realignment has occurred in steps. First, at the presidential level, in the 1980 election of Republican Ronald Reagan as president, and at the congressional or state level in 1994. Political analyst Kevin Phillips referred to this concept as "creeping" realignment.[8] The election of George Bush to the presidency in 2000 could be considered realignment except that the Republicans lost control of the senate by one vote.

Geographic Democratic and Republican Distribution

In the 1978 election for governor, Republican Bill Clements defeated Democrat John Hill. This was the first time since 1870 that Texas elected a Republican governor. Incumbent Republican U.S. Senator John Tower was also reelected in this election. Republicans were most successful in a very discernible stretch of territory that begins with Aransas County on the coast, crosses Texas in an almost unbroken path through the German Hill Country, the Edwards Plateau ranching area, and the oil-rich Permian Basin, and then checkerboards through West Texas and the southern Panhandle until almost total Republican domination is apparent in the ten northernmost Panhandle counties. The East Texas oil, commercial, and industrial counties (Smith, Gregg, and Rusk), the Dallas-Fort Worth area, and the Houston area display islands of Republican domination surrounded by an almost unbroken sea of Democrats. The greatest numbers of Republicans are in the urban-suburban areas in and around Dallas-Fort Worth and Houston.

Democratic strength is concentrated in South Texas, the area between Houston and the German Hill Country, and the Gulf Coast. There is also an almost unbroken pattern of Democratic domination in East, Central, and West Texas, and in the southeastern part of the Panhandle.

Figure 4.2 shows the turnaround in Republican strength in Texas in the 1990s and beyond. In the 2000 presidential election, the figure shows counties carried by the Republicans. In the 1990s Republicans have been successful throughout the state of Texas. It is now a situation of an almost unbroken sea of Republicans in which a few islands of Democratic dominance stand out. The most notable area of Democratic party strength is in Deep South Texas and counties along the Mexican border, which contain large Mexican-American populations, and a few counties in East and West Texas. The Democrats lost every major metropolitan county. In less than ten years, there has been a complete reversal of the position of party prevalence between Democrats and Republicans in Texas.

Party Organization

Party organization in the United States can be conceptualized as a pyramid in which the numbers of a party's organizations diminish with each step up until, at the apex, there is only one. In Texas the party hierarchy follows this pattern.

1. Voting precinct—There are at least several and often scores of these political divisions in each county, for the convenience of the voter and to simplify the administration of elections.

2. County or senatorial district—The county is the basic organizational entity. The senatorial district is used in urban counties that contain more than one

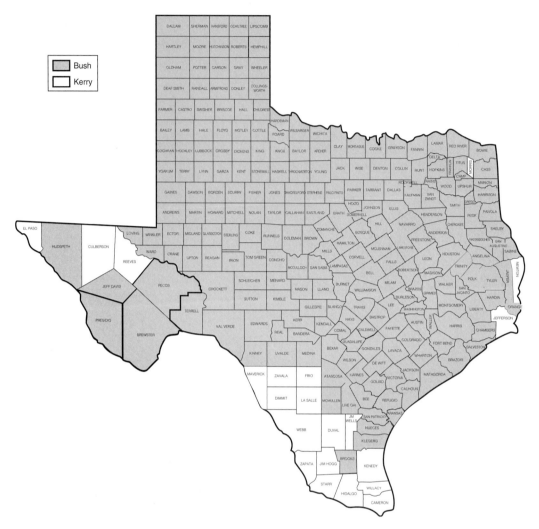

FIGURE 4.2 How Texas Voted for President, 2000

SOURCE: Federal Election Commission, www.fec.gov.

district, in order to keep county conventions from becoming too large and unwieldy.

3. The state—Because the principle of federalism requires that candidates be nominated from each state, their boundaries serve as a convenient organizational unit.

4. The national.

For further classification, party organizations are also separated into two categories based on the longevity of their active existence. Because conventions meet, conduct their business, and then disband, the party's series of conventions at the various geopolitical divisions are known collectively as the *temporary organization*. The elected party officers and committees that conduct the party's

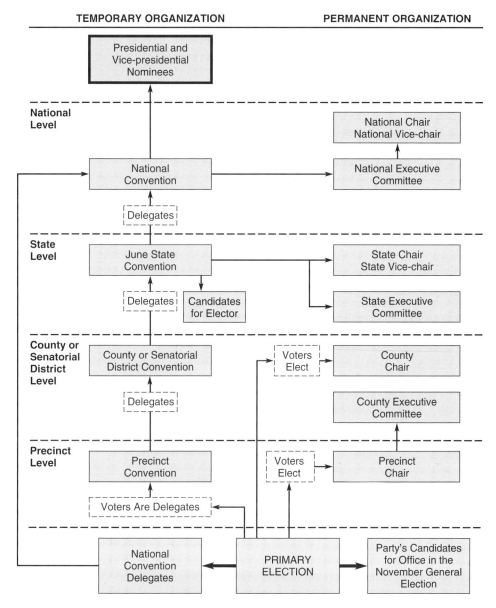

FIGURE 4.3 Texas Political Party Organization

affairs between conventions and meet from time to time on a continuing basis are labeled the *permanent organization* (see Figure 4.3).

The Temporary Party Organization

The Voting Precinct The delegates to the initial party convention are drawn from the voting precinct. The precinct convention is held on the second Tuesday in March of even numbered years, the day of the party's primary. Delegates may include any person who voted that day in that party's primary and thus established party membership. Actually, few attend. The order of business for the precinct convention is as follows:

1. A list of delegates is compiled, and support for a party faction or (in presidential campaign years) preference for a nominee for president is recorded.

2. A convention chairperson and secretary are elected.

3. Resolutions are adopted and forwarded to the next-level convention, where they may or may not be considered.

4. Delegates to the county or senatorial district convention are selected.

For the Democratic Party the makeup of this convention is determined by the percentage of precinct delegates that supported a particular candidate or faction when the convention first convened. Each faction or candidate group is allotted a percentage of the delegation to the next-level convention, equal to its share of representation in the precinct convention. Any group or faction that does not have at least 15 percent of the delegate representation is not given further representation. Each precinct is allotted one delegate for each twenty-five votes cast for that party's nominee for governor in the last general election. The Republican Party uses the "winner-take-all" concept, in which the majority group receives all the delegates.

The County or District Conventions   County or district conventions are held on the second Saturday following the precinct conventions. The basic format is the same as that of the precinct convention. However, county or district conventions are larger, longer, and more exciting.

The major function of the district or county convention is to select delegates who represent the various factions of the party at the state conventions. Each county or district convention is allotted one delegate for every three hundred votes cast in that county or district for the party's nominee for governor in the previous general election.

The State Conventions   Both the Democratic and Republican parties in Texas hold state conventions in June of even-numbered years. The major functions of these conventions are

1. To elect state party officials

2. To elect the sixty-two members of the state executive committee from their senatorial districts

3. To adopt a party platform

4. To certify to the secretary of state the candidates nominated by the party in its March primary.

In presidential election years, the state convention also performs the following functions:

1. To select some of the delegates to the national convention (most are selected by the presidential primary results)

2. To nominate (choose) the Texas party's membership on the National Executive Committee

3. To approve resolutions that will be submitted to the national convention

4. To nominate the Texas party's candidates for electors, who will cast their votes for the party's nominees for president and vice president should the nominees win a plurality in the general election.

The Permanent Party Organization   The permanent party organization consists of those offices and committees that help to administer the primaries, provide continuity for the party, and conduct the party's business between conventions. The geopolitical structure of the permanent organization, like that of the temporary organization, is divided along precinct, county, state, and national lines.

The Voting Precinct   The voting precinct has only one party official, the *precinct chair*, who is elected for a two-year term by the voters in the party primary. The duties of the chairperson may include serving as party organizer and helping to plan and conduct the primary elections and the precinct conventions. Most precinct chairpersons in Texas do little or nothing, and many of the positions are vacant.

The County   The party's permanent organization in each county consists of a *county chair* and a *county executive committee*. The executive committee is composed of all the party's precinct chairs in the county. The major functions of the executive committee are

1. To canvass the returns and certify the winners of the primary for local offices

2. To help prepare, with the county chair, the primary ballot and to determine the order of the candidates' names on the ballot.

The county chair is elected in the party's primary for a two-year term. The county chairperson serves as the unabashed supporter of the party both during and between elections. The chair also

1. Presides over the executive committee

2. Selects the polling places and election judges for the primary

3. Accepts fees or petitions from candidates for the party's nominations

4. Is responsible for the printing of paper ballots, and renting of voting machines

5. Submits the winners of the primary to the county executive committee for certification, and then transmits the official list of party nominees to the office of the secretary of state.

The State   The permanent party organization at the state level consists of a state chairperson and vice-chairperson of the opposite sex, and one man and one woman for each of the thirty-one state senatorial districts. The delegates at the state convention choose the chair and vice-chair for two-year terms. A caucus of the state convention delegates from their district chooses the other sixty-two members of the executive committee.

The chair presides over the executive committee, serves as temporary chair of the state convention, places statewide candidates on the primary ballot, and certifies the nomination of statewide candidates to the state convention. He or she also certifies to the secretary of state the candidates nominated in the primaries. The primary duties of the executive committee are to determine the site of the next state convention, and conduct party business between conventions.

LIBERALISM AND CONSERVATISM

The three political categories in which Texans tend to place themselves are *moderate, conservative,* and *liberal.* Although these labels are freely tossed around in political campaigns and barbershops, defining them is always difficult.

The problem has to do with perception. An individual who takes a position on a specific issue may consider that position middle-of-the-road (moderate). Other individuals may view the position as conservative, liberal, or whatever. As with most political matters, classification is largely a matter of opinion. The conservative and liberal positions will be the ones examined most closely here; the moderate position can generally be viewed as somewhere in between the other two.

How, then, may liberals and conservatives be defined? Plano and Greenburg use the following definitions:

Liberalism—A political view that seeks to change the political, economic, or social status quo to foster the development and well being of the individual. Liberals regard man as a rational creature who can use his intelligence to overcome human and natural obstacles to a good life for all without resorting to violence against the established order. Liberalism is more concerned with process, with the method of solving problems, than with a specific program.

Conservatism—Defense of the status quo against major changes in the political, economic, or social institutions of a society. The English statesman Edmund Burke expounded the classic statement of the philosophy of conservatism. He held that political stability could be maintained only if the forces of change could be moderated by a slow and careful integration of new elements into time-tested institutions.[9]

But what do these labels mean in terms of present political issues? The ambiguity of the expressions becomes apparent when we examine issues such as individual *liberty.* The liberal might clearly defend the rights of individuals to behave as they see fit, without governmental restraints, as long as the rights of others are not infringed. On the other hand, the conservative would probably encourage government restraint of individual behavior that is deviant or violates established ethics and norms of society. The liberal would advocate due-process rights for those charged with criminal acts and would take a strong position on the concept of "innocent until proven guilty." The conservative would be less sympathetic to judicial due process, especially if the accused is perceived to be guilty. This division has deepened with the restrictions on due process created by the War on Terrorism. On the other hand, liberals would not hesitate to use the power of government to restrain individual or corporate economic freedom for what they perceive as the general good. Conservatives, however, strongly oppose government restraints on corporate or individual economic freedom.

Taxing and spending are other areas in which liberal and conservative positions are diametrically opposed. Yet, again, it is difficult to simplify their positions. Although neither likes taxes, both conservatives and liberals realize that taxes are necessary to operate the institutions and programs of government. The basic difference of opinion has to do with what should be taxed, and how much. The liberal is more likely to favor taxes based on ability to pay. In other words, those who benefit most from our economic, social, and political systems should shoulder the greatest tax burden.

Conservatives argue that everyone benefits from our institutions, and if some benefit more than others, that is simply the way it is. To tax some more than others, based solely on their success, could stifle ambition and the desire to produce, and could ultimately destroy the free-enterprise system. Furthermore, everyone derives benefits from government, so everyone should pay generally equal taxes if there is to be any element of fair play in our tax system.

Conservatives also consider tax subsidies to corporations or business owners as being necessary to stimulate the economy, encourage commerce and manufacturing, encourage investments, and expedite business transactions. Liberals view these tax advantages as "loopholes" that are "welfare for the rich," written so the poor and middle class (those whom liberals claim are most in need of tax relief) cannot use them. Liberals further contend that these loopholes siphon treasury income that must be replaced by middle- and lower-income taxpayers.

Government *spending* is another major area of contention between liberals and conservatives. Neither particularly opposes spending, but both draw their ideological lines based on the purpose of the expenditure and the depth and breadth of its implementation. For example, liberals tend to support increased government expenditures for education, health services, social welfare programs, parks, and consumer, agricultural, and financial cooperatives. Conservatives encourage increased government spending for defense, police and fire protection, highways, and reservoir construction. They also favor direct subsidies to various aspects of commerce, industry, and business.

Usually neither liberals nor conservatives want to eliminate the programs favored by the other; instead, conflict arises over the *priorities* of government spending. For example, can government better combat violent crime by attacking the causes of crime—ignorance, poverty, and hopelessness? Or can government better protect its citizens and deter violent crime through the use of larger police forces, better equipment, more jails and prisons, and more vigorous prosecutions? Attitudes toward white-collar crime also differ. Liberals feel that white-collar criminals should be prosecuted vigorously, while conservatives argue that the loss of position and public disgrace that accompany exposure are punishment enough.

Liberals believe that there should be few restrictions concerning movies attended and books or magazines read by adults. They further advocate minimal restrictions on sexual behavior among consenting adults. Conversely, conservatives argue on the grounds that excessive individual freedom in these areas corrupts all society and will ultimately lead to America's decline and fall. Conservatives feel that exercise of these individual rights undercuts traditional family values.

Liberals tend to favor increased rights for African Americans, Mexican Americans, and women, even if it means implementing affirmative-action programs. Conservatives generally oppose affirmative action, believing instead that people should be hired and promoted on "merit." Conservatives, in order to preserve the traditional family and curb juvenile delinquency, tend to uphold the woman's traditional role as wife and homemaker. If work outside the home is necessary, it should be in the areas of traditional female employment such as teaching, secretarial work, and nursing, and should be considered supplemental to the earnings of the male "breadwinner."

In the 1990s, political observers felt that both liberals and conservatives were moving toward their ideological extremes. The conservatives moved toward the religious right, while liberals went toward the multicultural left. The 2000 national election highlighted this trend by producing a virtual government stalemate, as voters sought to find the middle ground. George Bush lost the popular vote, but won the presidency on electoral votes by winning the disputed electoral votes of the state of Florida. Moderate Republican Senator Jim Jeffords of Vermont gave Democrats control of the U.S. Senate 50–49, when he became an Independent. The Republican majority in the House was reduced.

Executive and political editor of the *Texas Monthly,* Paul Burka, feels that this movement away from moderate political views has grave consequences. According to Burka, "It will mean a less temperate political climate, fewer voices for compromise, more pressure to demonize the other side, greater anger among the outs, greater self-righteousness among the ins, and more and more people who are alienated from the political process."[10]

Many political issues cannot be subjected to a liberal or conservative analysis, but instead involve questions of individual conscience. One example is the War on Terror. Should the government use every power it possesses in order to protect the nation from terrorists? Or, on the other hand, does unsupervised government power pose a greater threat to our individual freedoms than terrorist activities?

These questions cannot be answered by liberal or conservative philosophy, for they transcend ideological classifications. Yet they must be answered, and open political dialogue must answer them.

CAMPAIGNING

Informal Requirements

Although all offices list one or more formal requirements that must be met by a potential candidate, the informal factors usually serve as the real limitations. Successful politicians in Texas tend to be male, Anglo-American, and Protestant.

Having the proper image is also critical for the successful candidate. Candidates for major office almost always hire public-relations firms to help "build an image" that will be presented to the voters through the same advertising techniques used to sell any other product. For a candidate, "packaging" can include such basics as attire and where and how to make appearances. Promotional photographs and TV tapes are chosen carefully to display a favorable overall image. In Texas, get-togethers at ranches, law libraries, public buildings, and barbecues serve as good background for campaigns. A favorite image is that of a typical family man, with a wife and children, who is religious and at the same time prosperous, successful, well educated, and attuned to the needs of the people. In other words, a man who stands with the common man—but somehow stands taller.

Name recognition is also vital to the successful candidate. One of the major values of incumbency is that the voters simply know the name. Name recognition in other fields, such as sports or show business, often translates into success at the polls. Children or relatives of successful politicians may have an advantage with the voters. A candidate who merely has the same name as an historic person may have an advantage at the polls—for example, Texas's former state treasurers, Jesse James and Warren G. Harding. In 1994, it certainly did not hurt George Bush to have the same name as his father, former President George Bush.

Name recognition can also be purchased. Although this is expensive, all candidates must rely on advertisements for some name recognition and image building. Bumper stickers, yard signs, spot commercials on radio or television, billboards, and newspaper ads really do nothing more than advertise the candidate's name, face, and political slogan.

Probably the most important single requirement for success in campaigning is money. Although successful campaigns based on "shoe leather, sweat, and hand shakes" are conducted in rural or small geographic areas, possessing money or the ability to raise it is critical to any campaign in which large numbers of voters must be reached. A statewide campaign involves a major financial endeavor.

Issues

The issues that are of utmost importance to the candidate are usually those determined by a poll taken to find out what the people want from a candidate. The candidate can then tell the people what they want to hear. Candidates choose only a small number of issues so as not to confuse the voters; these issues are emphasized over and over throughout the campaign. The key issues of the twenty-first century burst suddenly on the political landscape in 2001. The terrorist attack of September 11, 2001, along with the loss of the government budget surplus, produced the issues of national security and the economy as top priorities.

At the state and local level, issues often are secondary and personal attacks on opponents comprise the major thrust of the campaign. Attempts are made to create negative images of other candidates in the minds of the voters by using such phrases as "professional politician," "liberal," "supported by big-money interests," and "supported by labor."

Campaign Assistance

Candidates often ask for help from other politicians or sports and show business stars, who may appear in person or simply allow the use of their names and photographs on campaign literature. The candidate must be careful, however, to choose people who create a positive image in the minds of the voters. Former President Clinton's current lack of popularity in Texas, for example, would make him a risky choice for Democratic candidates.

Polls

Polls are becoming increasingly important as campaigns become more costly. In addition to providing information about the issues, they can also reveal the candidate's relative strengths or weaknesses with various groups and show how well he or she compares with other candidates. A candidate, who claims that the polls show he or she is leading, can also use them as propaganda. Opponents, whose polls may in fact show the opposite trend, may dispute these claims.

Media

Of all the aspects of campaigning, the use of media has become the most critical. Today, no candidate for a major state or national office can be elected without the skillful use of broadcast media—radio and television.

Advertising on radio and television is very expensive today, and that is one of the key reasons for the high cost of campaigning for public office. For example, in 1990, Republican Clayton Williams, while spending a reported $20 million, lost to Democrat Ann Richards, who spent almost $12 million.[11] This campaign was unusual because the candidate spending the most money almost always wins. The key factor in Williams's loss seems to have been a number of public statements that the inexperienced candidate Williams made, including one comparing rape to the Texas weather.[12] George W. Bush spent $15 million to defeat Governor Richards in 1994. In 1996, Republican incumbent Phil Gramm spent $6.2 million in defeating Democrat Victor Morales for the U.S. Senate. In 2002, Democrat Tony Sanchez spent $70 million, and still lost to Governor Rick Perry, who only spent about $30 million. Races for lesser statewide offices require at least $1 million or more. The size of the state of Texas is a major reason for the high cost of running for public office. Texas has 27 media markets in which a statewide candidate must purchase time on radio and television. In 2000, the rates in just one market, Houston, could run from $1,500 to $25,000 for one 30-second "spot" on one station. You can imagine the total media cost for all the stations in all the media markets in the state! In the 2004 congressional elections, Texas had three of the top ten most expensive elections.[13]

The cost of campaigning for public office increases with each election, and it is becoming obvious that only wealthy individuals or individuals who can raise large sums of money from organized groups can have a realistic chance to win public office.

CONCLUSION

Concerned about societal problems, individual citizens will seek to maximize their political influence by joining interest groups. Business and professions, as well as labor unions and agriculture, have traditionally organized to represent their interests. In recent years, groups concerned with traditional religious values and with environmental issues have become more important. These groups have used lobbyists and the creation of political action committees (PACs) to make campaign contributions in an attempt to influence public policy.

Political parties take over where interest groups leave off, by recruiting candidates and developing issues that seek to appeal to interest-group concerns. Parties also play a major role in the election process by facilitating the campaigning process and getting the vote out.

Unlike many states, the Democratic Party in Texas has dominated the political process for a number of years. From the Civil War period to the 1960s in Texas, political party competition was between liberal and conservative Democrats, because Texas was a one-party state. In the 1970s, the Republican Party began to develop strength, as conservative Democrats began to vote for Republican candidates for president. This created "presidential Republicans." The growth of Republican Party strength continued in the 1980s and 1990s.

In the 1994 elections, the Republican Party achieved parity with the Democrats. The Republican Party gained control of Congress at the national level for the first time in over forty years. In Texas, the Republican Party elected the governor, one U.S. Senator, and record numbers of statewide officials and members of the Texas legislature.

In the 2002 elections, the Republican Party achieved domination of the political process in Texas. Republicans swept to victory in statewide elections, lead by Governor Rick Perry. Republicans captured control of the Legislature by winning 88 of the 150 seats in the Texas House and 19 of 31 seats in the Texas Senate. In the 2004 elections, this trend continued as Republicans won 87 of 150 seats in the Texas House and retained 19 of 31 seats in the Texas Senate.

Ideology, political parties, and wealth have all made an impact on the institutions of government in Texas. In the next chapter, these influences on the legislative branch are examined.

KEY TERMS

conservatism	liberalism	state convention
county or senatorial district	lobbying	voting precinct
interest groups	political action committees	

Logging On

For a look at the Web sites of leading economic interest groups in Texas, go to Texas Trial Lawyers' Association at **http://www.ttla.com/,** Texas Farm Bureau at **http://www.fb.com/txfb/index.html,** Texas AFL-CIO at **http://www.texasaflcio.org**. To find out how much money political action committees (PACs) gave to the campaign of your congressperson, go to the Federal Election Commission at **http://www.fec.gov/**. Click on financial information about candidates, parties, and PACs. The two major political parties in Texas are on the Web: Democrats at **http://www.txdemocrats.org/**. Republicans at **http://www.texasgop.org**.

ENDNOTES

1. Jeffrey Berry, *The Interest Group Society* (Boston: Little, Brown, and Company), 1984, p. 65.

2. R. G. Ratcliffe and Diana Williams, "Ethics Bill Skirts Limit on PACs," *Houston Chronicle,* March 2, 1991.

3. Federal Election Commission Web site, http://fec.gov, Major provisions of the Bipartisan Campaign Reform Act of 2002.

4. Walter Dean Burnham, *The Current Crisis in American Politics* (New York: Oxford University Press), 1982, p. 110.

5. Gardner Selby, "Top Issue for New Faces on Education Board," *The Houston Post,* Thursday, November 10, 1994.

6. *San Antonio Express-News,* Wednesday, Nov. 9, 1994, p. 18A.

7. Kevin Phillips, *Post-Conservative America* (New York: Vantage Books), 1983, p. 221.

8. Ken Herman, "Republicans, Bush Savor Wins Flavor," *The Houston Post,* Thursday, November 10, 1994, p. 1.

9. Jack C. Plano and Milton Greenberg, *The American Political Dictionary,* 5th ed. (Hinsdale, IL: The Dryden Press), 1987.

10. Paul Burka, "Stuck in the Middle," *Texas Monthly* (November 1994), Volume 22–Issue 11, p. 85.

11. Sue Tolleson-Rinehart and Jeanie Stanley, *Claytie and the Lady* (Austin: Univ. of Texas Press), 1994, p. 67.

12. Tolleson-Rinehart and Stanley, p. 102.

13. Center for Responsive Politics, http://www.opemsecrets.org.

5

The Texas Legislature: Organization and Processes

INTRODUCTION

Legislative bodies pass laws, and it is by law that government policy is made, spending priorities are established, and public programs are created. The executive branch has the responsibility to carry out or implement public policy. For example, the legislative branch defines crime, but the executive branch arrests, prosecutes, and punishes criminals. While the legislative branch determines who will pay how much in taxes, the executive branch actually collects them. The legislative branch passes appropriations bills and sets spending priorities, but the executive branch lets the contacts and writes the checks. The legislative branch decides which programs and services will be provided, but the executive branch actually provides those services, hires the personnel, and manages their day-to-day conduct. The legislative branch decides *what the government will do; the executive branch actually does it.*

Most state governors use their patronage power (to appoint supporters to high-level positions), control over a budget, access to publicity, and leadership of their party to become dominant figures. In Texas, however, traditional fear of executive power instead makes the legislature and its leaders extraordinarily powerful, and they have even assumed some roles traditionally reserved to the executive, such as proposing a state budget.

The Texas legislature, like the U.S. Congress and all other state legislatures except Nebraska's, is a bicameral (two-house) legislature composed of a senate and a house of representatives. Although the two houses formally have approximately equal power, the smaller, 31-member senate is more prestigious, and its individual members exercise greater influence than the 150 members of the house of representatives.

GEOGRAPHIC DISTRICTS

Texas legislators are elected from single-member districts (one member per district) that are approximately equal in population, as required by a U.S. Supreme Court ruling in the early 1960s.[1] This ruling, known as the "one man, one vote" decision, held that each legislator in a state's legislative body should represent an equal number of people. The average population for each of the 150 districts for members of the house is about 140,000; the average population in each of the 31 senatorial districts is roughly 677,000. The legislature redraws boundary lines for these districts in the first regular session after each ten-year census, in order to maintain equal distribution of population among districts. When the legislature fails to act, as it did in its 2001 session, the state constitution provides that the Legislative Redistricting Board (consisting of the lieutenant governor, speaker of the house, attorney general, comptroller of public accounts, and commissioner of the general land office) draws new legislative district lines. Figures 5.1 and 5.2 show Texas's current house and senate districts.

The Texas legislature also draws boundaries for the state's thirty-two U.S. congressional districts, which must also be apportioned according to the "one person,

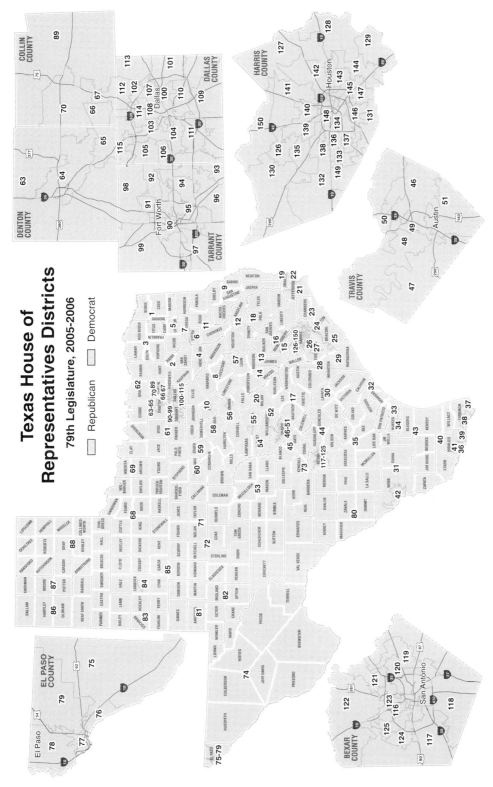

FIGURE 5.1 Texas House of Representatives Districts, 79th Legislature, 2005–2006

SOURCE: Texas Legislative Council.

81

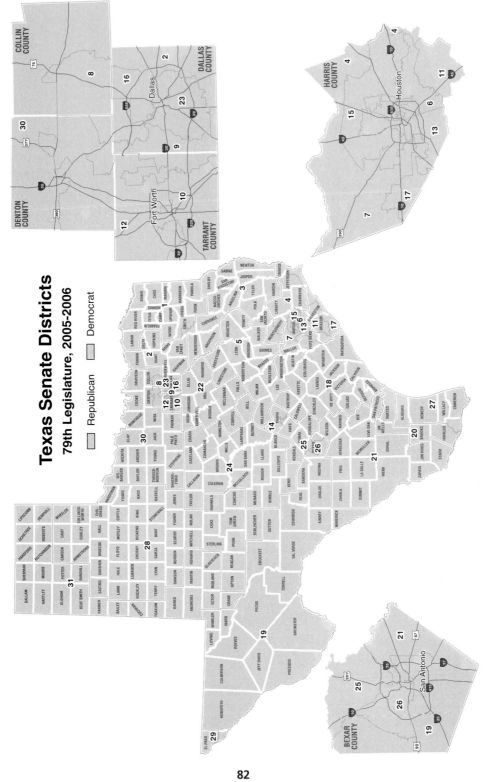

Texas Senate Districts
79th Legislature, 2005–2006

Republican

Democrat

FIGURE 5.2 Texas Senate Districts, 79th Legislature, 2005–2006

SOURCE: Texas Legislative Council.

one vote" principle.[2] Malapportioned legislative and congressional districts (of substantially unequal population) have been eliminated, but districts are still subject to *gerrymandering* (the drawing of legislative district lines to reduce representation of political minorities). Only racial or ethnic gerrymandering is forbidden by the Fifteenth Amendment and the federal Voting Rights Act of 1965 and its later amendments.

Three basic gerrymander techniques are generally used. One is to diffuse a concentrated political or ethnic minority among several districts so that its votes within any one district are negligible. If the minority's numbers are great enough when diffused to affect the outcome of elections in several districts, the minority is instead concentrated or "packed" within one district, thereby assuring that it will influence only one election and that its influence within the whole legislature will be minimal. A third tactic is a pairing technique that locates the residences and/or political bases of two or more incumbent legislators and redistricts them into the same district— thereby assuring that one will be defeated. Pairing is often used to punish legislators who have fallen from grace with the legislative leadership.

Gerrymandering is a perpetual political and legal issue for the Texas legislature. The Republican-dominated Redistricting Board successfully increased their party's members in the legislature from 48 to 59 percent after the 2002 elections. In 2003, Governor Perry called three special legislative sessions to redraw the state's 32 U.S. congressional district boundaries to favor Republicans. As a result, Republican members of the U.S. Congressional delegation increased from 15 to 22.

QUALIFICATIONS FOR MEMBERSHIP

Formal Qualifications

Although legal or formal qualifications must be met before anyone can serve in the legislature, rarely do such requirements prohibit serious candidates from seeking legislative seats. In fact, the criteria are broad enough to allow millions of Texans to run for the legislature. To be a Texas senator, an individual must be a U.S. citizen, a qualified voter, at least twenty-six years of age, and must have lived for five years in the state and one year in the district in which the person is seeking election.

Qualifications for the house of representatives are even more easily met. A candidate must be a U.S. citizen, a qualified voter, at least twenty-one years of age, and must have lived in Texas for two years and in the district for one year.

Informal Qualifications

The most important requirements for holding legislative office in Texas, however, are not the formal qualifications. Instead, there are a number of informal political, social, and economic factors that largely determine who will be elected, not only to the legislature, but to most other offices as well.

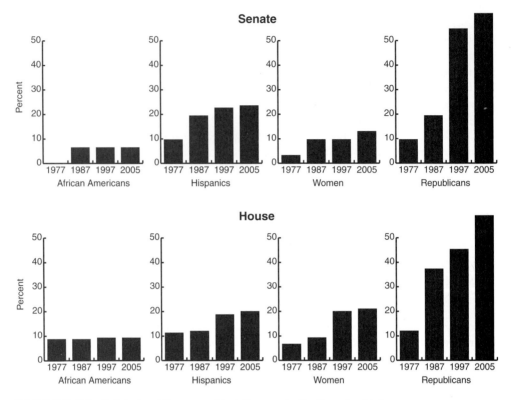

FIGURE 5.3 Political and Demographical Changes in the Texas Legislature

SOURCE: Texas Legislative Reference Library (http://www.lrl.state.tx.us/).

Party, Religion, Race, and Gender   For decades, the Texas legislature has been dominated by conservative, Anglo-American, male Protestants. In most parts of the state, a candidate possessing these characteristics has had an edge over other candidates. Figure 5.3 illustrates recent political and demographic changes in the Texas legislature. Ethnic minorities and women have been elected in larger numbers in recent years. By 2005, African Americans and Hispanics almost reflect their percentage in the adult Texas population. Women (who are only 19.3 percent of the legislature's 181 members) are the most underrepresented of these groups compared to the state's population as a whole.

Historically, the Texas legislature was dominated by moderate and conservative Democrats. More recently, Republicans have been making steady and dramatic gains and by 2005, Republicans controlled 61 percent of the state senate and 57 percent of the house seats. The most important political event in modern Texas political history has been the rise of the Republican Party to dominance of state government.

Occupation   Because of the length of the legislative session and the low salaries, Texas legislators must function on a part-time basis. Thus, when the session adjourns, the typical legislator returns home to earn a living at his or her chosen profession. Between 5,000 and 10,000 professions are represented in the legislature, but most members are businesspersons or lawyers, with a sprinkling of farmers or ranchers and other professions.

The overrepresentation of persons involved in business gives the legislature a "free-enterprise," conservative perspective. The legislators who are attorneys often face a conflict of interest because it is difficult for lawyer-legislators to separate the public interest from the interests of those paying them large retainers. Meanwhile, other occupational groups and their perspectives are not well represented in the legislature.

SESSIONS AND SALARIES

The Texas legislature meets in regular 140-day sessions beginning in January in odd-numbered years. Of the ten most populous states, only the Texas legislature meets biennially (every two years). In fact, only six state legislatures do not meet in regular annual sessions.

With such a short time in which to work, legislators are overwhelmed by the sheer volume of legislation. Between 5,000 and 9,000 bills and resolutions are introduced in the typical legislative session. In the 2005 regular session, 9,338 pieces of legislation were introduced. Many of these were of negligible importance to the general public (resolutions to honor legislators, resolutions to honor certain "prominent" citizens, and so forth). Most were passed or killed with little consideration, but they consumed valuable time that could have been used more effectively, and many important bills were never granted a legislative hearing.

In addition to regular sessions scheduled by the state constitution, special sessions may be called by the governor, who also sets their agendas. Special sessions are limited to thirty days and, although the governor may officially call as many special sessions as he or she chooses, there is a practical limit on the number of special sessions. Special sessions cost at least $800,000, with some costing millions, and taxpayers are likely to view the governor as wasteful if he or she uses this particular gubernatorial prerogative too often. Public opinion was aroused when several special sessions in 2004 and 2005 failed to pass school property tax reform. Legislators resent frequent calls to Austin that take them away from their hometowns, families, and primary occupations, and may react unfavorably toward the governor's proposals.

As most of the legislative work is done during the regular session, time becomes vital. The over-worked legislator finds it increasingly difficult to maintain even rudimentary knowledge about much of the legislation that must be considered, whether in committee or on the floor of the house. A more serious drain on legislative time is caused by the processing of bills that are limited in scope or deal with trivia (for example, the size of melon containers or the regulation of minnow seining in a specific county). Although they affect public policy, these bills are important only to a limited number of people and could easily be delegated to an appropriate department or agency in the executive branch.

The limited biennial session tends to work against good legislative practice and ultimately harms the public interest. Texas legislators cannot possibly acquaint themselves with the immense volume of legislation in only 140 days, even though the work is divided in the committee system. Few legislators have specialized knowledge about a given subject unless they are employed or hold investment interests in that particular field. The short session denies legislators sufficient time for deliberate, comprehensive research into the state's problems and the proposals made by special-interest groups.

An example of vital legislation that demands calm deliberation by the elected representatives of Texas is the state appropriations bill, which has far-reaching consequences in all aspects of state government. In 2005 the state legislature appropriated $139 billion to cover the state's expenditures for 2006–07. The biennial session, together with an unpredictable economy, makes it particularly difficult for legislators to rationally appropriate funds for state government. Texans expect their legislators to fund state government for twenty-four months in advance when it is impossible to predict accurately expenses such as how many students will enroll in the state's community colleges and universities, how many inmates will be sentenced to state penitentiaries, how many patients will be sent to state mental and tuberculosis hospitals, how many will become eligible for Medicaid and unemployment compensation, or how many potholes will develop along state highways. Although other populous states have annual sessions for conducting state business, Texans believe that the legislature does more harm than good when it is in session and consistently refuses to adopt either annual or longer sessions.

Legislators receive an annual salary of $7,200, plus $125 for each day of the regular session and any special sessions the governor might call. The state ethics commission sets the per diem allowance, but it may only recommend an increase in base salary, which must be approved by voters. Figure 5.4 compares legislative salaries and sessions in the fifty states.

Low pay forces legislators to spend most of their time and energy earning a living by their other occupational endeavors and makes it impossible for most legislators to dedicate much time to studying state issues. They must depend heavily on lobbyists for information on key legislative proposals and sometimes resort to questionable sources to supplement their incomes.

TERMS AND TURNOVER

In Texas, state senators are elected for a term of four years, and members of the house for a two-year term. The entire house and half the senate is elected every two years. As in other states, many factors contribute to a turnover in legislators that is higher than that in the U.S. Congress, with turnover rates especially high after redrawing of state district boundaries following the census every ten years. Twenty-four percent of Texas legislators were freshmen following redistricting after the 2000 census; by 2005 only 9 percent were first-time members.

Inexperienced legislators are generally amateurish at lawmaking. Short sessions, heavy workloads, and the lack of adequate staff and clerical assistance

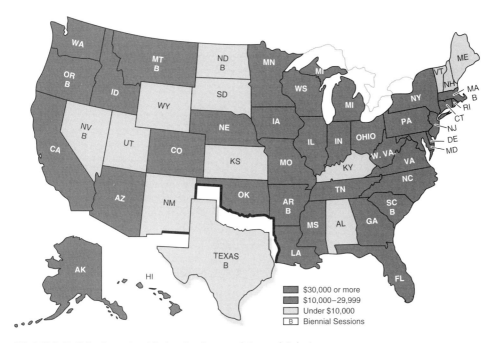

FIGURE 5.4 State Legislative Sessions and Annual Salaries

SOURCE: Data from *The Book of the States, 2004* (Lexington, KY: Council of State Governments, 2004), pp. 78–81, 94–96.

diminish the legislators' effectiveness and render them dependent on lobbyists for information. This is compounded by the legislator's feeling of impotence with respect to achieving legislative goals when the legislator confronts the power of either powerful interest groups or the presiding officers. The low legislative salaries are a major concern. The relatively low esteem in which state legislators are held by the public also causes many to leave office. Some may seek higher political office, either to satisfy political ambition, improve their incomes, or achieve increased social or political prestige. Many become lobbyists and others retire to private life. Whatever its causes, this high turnover rate results in poor legislative procedure and a lack of expert and independent judgment concerning administrative and interest-group requests. All these factors lead to inferior representation for the legislators' constituents.

THE PRESIDING OFFICERS

By far the most visible and powerful individuals in the Texas legislature are the two presiding officers: the lieutenant governor in the senate and the speaker of the house of representatives. In the past, the presiding officers have acted in a nonpartisan or bipartisan fashion. Now, they represent the overwhelming Republican majority party.

Appointing a few Democrats to important committee positions is little more than a token gesture. There has been a clear realignment of voters in Texas elections toward the Republicans and the legislature's leaders usually comply with the wishes of those who financed their campaigns and the voters who elected them.

The Lieutenant Governor

The presiding officer and dominant figure in the Texas senate is the lieutenant governor, who serves as its president. The lieutenant governor is elected in a statewide election for a four-year term; this election is usually overshadowed by the governor's race, even though the lieutenant governor is one of the most powerful officials in Texas government. Organized interest groups usually contribute sizeable sums to ensure that their favorite is elected. The senators have adopted rules that grant the lieutenant governor extensive legislative powers, including organizational, procedural, administrative, and planning authority.

In most other states, lieutenant governors are akin to the U.S. vice president, neither strong executives nor strong legislative leaders. Several states have eliminated the lieutenant governor's office altogether, or require governor and lieutenant governor to run as a team like the U.S. president and vice president. In these states, the governor and other executives monopolize the executive function, and the upper house, where the lieutenant governor usually presides, is often too jealous of its legislative powers to include him or her in the real power structure. Although many lieutenant governors exercise a hybrid executive-legislative function, probably no lieutenant governor is so powerful as the one in Texas.

The Speaker of the House

The house of representatives, by a majority vote of its membership, chooses its presiding officer from among its members. Although a potential speaker must win the support of thousands of voters to become a representative, the real battle is for the critical seventy-six votes in the house.

The campaign for this important position is usually very low-key, but often begins years in advance of the actual election. Several members, after announcing themselves as candidates for speaker, set about gaining pledges of support from other members. The campaign is based on personal loyalties and an understanding the supporters of the winning candidate for speaker will be part of the "team" and receive important committee assignments. Funds raised and spent during the campaign for the speakership are limited and are a matter of the public record; candidates must file a complete statement, which details loans, campaign contributions, and expenditures.

THE LEGISLATIVE COMMITTEES

Because of the immense volume of legislative proposals each session, legislators cannot possibly become familiar with all bills, not even all the major ones. They divide themselves into various committees, thus providing a very necessary division

AP/Wide World Photos

Texas Speaker of the House Tom Craddick is the center of political power in the house of representatives.

of labor and ensuring that at least someone knows something about the legislation under consideration.

Types of Committees

There are several types of legislative committees.

1. *Standing committees* are permanent and initially consider most bills.

2. *Subcommittees* are a further division of standing committees; they consider issues within their areas of specialization.

3. *Ad hoc committees* are temporary committees appointed to consider special issues or problems.

4. *Conference committees* are compromise committees that resolve differences between bills passed by both houses in different forms.

5. *Interim committees* meet when the legislature is not in session and consider proposed legislation for the next legislative session or study a particular problem that has arisen since the last session.

Standing committees and subcommittees are the basic subdivisions found in the Texas legislature. They are organized much like the senate and house, each with a presiding officer, a chair, and a vice chair. Each legislator serves on at least one committee; some serve on several. Among standing committees are subject-matter or substantive committees that examine the content of a bill, holding hearings and often rewriting it. Meanwhile, procedural committees manage the legislative process, writing rules and scheduling bills for final action.

A committee's membership is sometimes further divided into subcommittees with their own chairs. The subcommittee members are usually among the first legislators to become familiar with a bill and report their findings to the whole standing committee

The Texas house of representatives has forty-three committees and six subcommittees on appropriations. Members cannot serve concurrently on more than two substantive committees, but they may serve on an additional procedural committee. The chairs of the House Appropriations Committee and State Affairs Committee cannot serve on other substantive committees. The senate has only sixteen committees with three standing subcommittees.

THE LEGISLATIVE STAFF

Although the voters set legislative salaries, legislators themselves appropriate most of the money for their expense accounts. House members receive over $7,500 per month for staff salaries and expenses. Senators get a staff salary allowance of over $22,000 per month and "reasonable and necessary" office expenses. These expense accounts are designated for office, staff, and clerical expenses, not for personal expenses. Some legislators have pooled their funds to create the House Research Organization. Additional assistance is available through the Legislative Council.

These legislative expense accounts may seem like a great deal of money, but neither individual legislators nor legislative committees have professional staff comparable to those employed by the lobbyists or the bureaucrats who target staff with at least as much energy as they dedicate to legislators. Because legislators function in an atmosphere where knowledge is power, inadequate staffing is a problem. If legislators are to make decisions relatively free of influence from interest-group propaganda, they must have competent, independent staffs that are as well-educated, highly trained, and highly motivated as the staffs of special-interest groups. Without such personnel, legislators and committees can be easily misled by the "expert" advice of interest groups and agency lobbyists.

Additional funding to provide adequate legislative assistance is becoming increasingly unlikely because of budget cuts and opposition by both the electorate and Texas interest groups, who want the legislature to remain dependent on them for information. Legislators who report a surplus in their expense accounts are often acclaimed by the press as conscientious guardians of the public treasury.

THE LEGISLATIVE PROCESS

The Powers of the Presiding Officers

To understand the Texas legislature, the student must realize the extent of the power exercised by the lieutenant governor in the senate and the speaker of the house of representatives—power that can be roughly divided into two general categories: procedural and institutional.

The rules of each house, either formally or informally, give the presiding officers the following procedural powers:

1. To appoint most committee members

2. To appoint committee chairs

3. To refer bills to committee

4. To schedule legislation for floor action

5. To recognize members on the floor for amendments and points of order

6. To interpret the procedural rules when conflict arises

7. To appoint the chairs and members of conference committees.

Laws or legislative rules grant the following institutional powers to the presiding officers:

1. To appoint the members and serve as chair (lieutenant governor) and vice-chair (speaker) of the Legislative Budget Board

2. To appoint the members and serve as chair (lieutenant governor) and vice-chair (speaker) of the Legislative Council

3. To appoint the members and serve as chair (lieutenant governor) and vice-chair (speaker) of the Legislative Audit Committee

4. To appoint the members and serve as members of the Sunset Advisory Commission

Procedural Tools of Leadership

Committee Membership   The committee is of great importance in the legislative process; therefore, those who determine membership of committees exercise considerable influence on their policy decisions. In Texas, this power belongs to the lieutenant governor and the speaker. Although the house of representatives uses a limited seniority system to determine up to one-half of a substantive committee's membership, the speaker appoints the other half and is able to "stack" important committees with supporters and friends. The speaker also appoints, without respect to seniority, all members of important procedural committees such as the Rules and Calendars Committees.

The lieutenant governor officially appoints the total membership of all senate committees; in practice, though, an informal seniority system ensures that up to one-third of the membership of the most powerful committees will be senior senators. The appointive power of the presiding officers means that the actions of a committee concerning specific legislation are usually predictable. The presiding officers can use the power of appointment to reward friends and supporters as well as to punish opponents. Interest groups often attempt to influence the presiding officer's selection of a committee's membership. (Interest groups need sympathetic members on a committee that reviews legislation important to their interests.) Membership on an important committee gives a legislator a greatly strengthened bargaining position with administrators, lobbyists, and other legislators.

Although there is no way to determine precisely all the coalitions, compromises, and bargains that can lead to a desirable committee appointment, it is generally accepted that among the more powerful committees in the house are Appropriations, Ways and Means, and State Affairs. Among the more powerful senate committees are Finance and State Affairs. Negotiations for committee positions are intense, and all legislative bodies experience conflict over committee appointments. Concentrating the power of committee selection in the office of the presiding officers is one way to resolve such conflict.

Selection of Committee Chairs   Because the chairs of legislative committees largely determine the ultimate success or failure of legislation, conflict over their selection is inevitable. In some states, committee chairs are selected by the majority of the committee; in others, the seniority system is used. In Texas the presiding officers of the legislature make these decisions. Due to their power over committees' organization, procedure, and the legislative jurisdiction of subcommittees, the fate of much legislation is determined when chairs are selected.

The presiding officers, by virtue of their power to appoint the chairs of all committees, have a tool like a magnet that attracts legislators to their "team." The rule is "If you want to get along, go along" (with the presiding officers). This power also increases the bargaining position of the presiding officers with respect to the interest groups. Lobbyists who can help get sympathetic legislators appointed as chairs of important committees have certainly earned the salary paid them by their employers. At the same time, lobbyists owe the presiding officer some favors for appointing the "right" committee chair.

The power of the presiding officers, although significant, is not absolute, and they often appoint key committee chairs who have political power in their own right. The presiding officers can then enjoy the support of some of the more powerful members of the legislature in a mutually beneficial relationship. The presiding officers can usually count on the loyalty of the chairs, and the chairs can, in turn, usually depend on support from the presiding officers. They sometimes even cross party lines in appointing committee chairs in an effort to win some support among potential opponents.

In contrast to the Texas appointive system, the U.S. congressional seniority system (in which the most senior member of the majority party on the committee is usually to the chairmanship) reduces the leadership's ability to maneuver and bargain with legislators and interest groups. The Texas legislature's presiding officers are more able to shape the content of legislation by choosing committee chairs and members with viewpoints similar to their own.

Committee Jurisdiction   The presiding officers in the Texas legislature are responsible for assigning bills to particular committees. Unlike the system in the U.S. Congress, in which committee jurisdiction over specific legislation is reasonably well established, committees in the Texas legislature often have overlapping jurisdiction; the presiding officers have considerable flexibility when assigning bills to committees. Texas presiding officers do not hesitate to assign a bill that they oppose to a committee that they know will give the bill unfavorable consideration, while sending bills they support to committees that support them. This is a simple procedure, as the presiding officers have shaped the committees to their liking.

Committee Powers and Functions   Each session, several thousand bills and resolutions are introduced in the Texas legislature and referred to standing committees. These committees are often called "little legislatures," because they have broad powers and conduct much of the business of the legislature. After a standing committee receives a bill, it may hold public hearings, at which witnesses (mostly lobbyists) testify for or against the proposal. The committee members can then discuss and debate the bill and vote on the question of whether it should be approved, modified, or killed by the committee. The committee may take a wide range of actions, ranging from approval as written, to a complete revision of the bill (mark-up), to no action at all (pigeonholing).

Committee members are often expected to gain some measure of competence in their subject-matter areas. This competence is important because committee members pondering a decision on a particular bill will usually hear arguments from competing interest groups, and perceptive questioning by knowledgeable committee members might shed light on the topic. The limited and informal seniority systems used to determine committee membership in the Texas legislature help to ensure that at least a few committee members have some background knowledge about their subject and an idea of which questions to ask.

Committees in the Texas legislature also serve as burying grounds for bills. A legislator may introduce a bill as a favor for some group or constituent, knowing full well that the bill will be killed in committee (and that the committee will take the blame). Bills may be assigned to a hostile committee, in which case they stand a very good chance of being totally rewritten, if not pigeonholed.

All legislative bodies have procedures by which bills can be extracted from reluctant committees, although this is usually a difficult process. Legislators feel that it is to their advantage to retain the powers of the committee system, and even though they may support a bill buried in a committee, they are reluctant to vote to discharge it. They see the discharge as a threat to the privileges of the whole committee system—privileges that they, too, enjoy.

Senate rules allow a procedure, known as "tagging," enabling any senator to require the chair of a senate committee to give that senator forty-eight hours' advance notice as to when the committee will hold hearings on a bill (thus, delaying the hearings for forty-eight hours). The tagging procedure is not debatable, and no committee action may be taken on the bill within that period. (If the bill's sponsors can get the senator to "remove the tag," the bill can be immediately cleared for committee hearings.) In effect, tagging enables a single senator to kill a bill late in the short legislative session.

The Calendar   Bills that have been reported favorably by the legislative committees must be scheduled for debate on the floor of the house considering the measure. This schedule, referred to as the *calendar,* theoretically ensures that measures will be brought up for debate in an orderly fashion. Different calendars are used, depending on whether the legislation is judged to be emergency, major, general, or trivial in nature.

Unimportant bills, or bills thought to affect only one town or area, are often placed on special calendars and passed promptly with little or no debate or attention. Major or controversial legislation, though, usually receives more debate and attention, and there are several reasons why its place on the calendar may have a significant effect on whether it passes.

1. Supporters may want floor consideration of the legislation delayed until they can gain the necessary votes to get the bill passed. (The opponents may feel that they have the necessary votes to defeat the bill, but their strength could erode if the supporters are given time to marshal their forces.)

2. Conversely, supporters may want an early consideration of the bill because the opposition appears to be gaining strength (opponents would want delay under these circumstances).

3. A bill that has been placed late on the calendar may be killed by opponents, even if they are in the minority, through the use of the filibuster, tagging, or other parliamentary maneuvers.

4. The legislature may never even consider the bill if it is placed too far down on the calendar. Although the desirability of either early or late consideration of legislation varies with the situation and parties involved, control of this stage in the life of a bill is a powerful weapon that can be used either to aid or hinder passage of the legislation, as well as to reward allies or punish enemies.

Control of the calendar of bills is especially important to the Texas legislature, which is saddled with limited, biennial sessions. The shorter and more rigid the legislative session, the more important are the political forces that control the agenda of legislation.

The House Calendars   In the house, a Committee on Calendars assigns bills to the various calendars. Bills passed by the various substantive committees go directly to this committee. Rules of the house require the Committee on Calendars to make the calendar assignment for each bill or vote to kill it within a specified time. The house itself can, by a majority vote, assign a bill to a calendar. The house calendars are (1) Emergency, (2) Major State, (3) Constitutional Amendments, (4) General State, (5) Local, Consent, and Resolutions, (6) Resolutions, and (7) Congratulatory and Memorial Resolutions.

Because the Committee on Calendars officially schedules legislation for action in the house, the speaker of the house has no formal control over the various house calendars. This may be a bit misleading, however, because the speaker appoints the entire membership of this committee and dominates its activities.

The Calendar of the Senate   In theory, senate bills are advanced systematically on the calendar in the order in which they are reported out of committee. In practice, a trivial bill (a "blocking bill") with little support is placed first on the senate calendar and other bills are taken up for debate out of sequence by a suspension of the rules, which requires a two-thirds vote. Ironically, while only a simple majority is necessary for passage of a bill, a two-thirds majority is necessary to bring a bill up for consideration on the floor. Because there are thirty-one members of the senate, a coalition of only eleven senators can effectively block floor action, and thus kill a piece of legislation. In the past, this has led to much head-counting and political maneuvering, and many bills have been passed by an opportunistic senator who noted that one or more of his foes were momentarily absent. Currently, senators who wish to bring a bill up for debate must file a "notice of intent" with the secretary of the senate on the day before such action is planned. A list of these bills is printed and distributed the next day, before the session begins. This "intent calendar," as it has come to be called, is the closest thing to an actual calendar in the senate.

The Floor of the House   As bills reach the floor of the house, a loudspeaker system allows the members and visitors to follow the debate on the floor. The floor leaders (representatives who are attempting to get the bill passed) usually stand at the front of the chamber, answer questions, and speak in favor of the bill. Microphones situated elsewhere in the House chamber allow either the opponents of the bill or other concerned lawmakers to speak against the bill or simply ask questions.

The consideration of bills on the floor of the house seems to be a study in confusion and inattention. Throughout the process, representatives may be laughing, talking, reading papers, or sleeping at their desks. Some members may already have a well-defined position on the bill under consideration, but others may know little of its content. Floor debate should be an excellent opportunity for both proponents and opponents to seek support for their positions. In practice, eloquent speeches and factual support seldom change votes. In fact, many members vote for or against legislation depending on who is supporting it or who is against it, and then they may ask what the bill was all about. This is especially true of specialized bills that have generated little statewide interest. When it is time to vote, supporters and opponents of the bill usually move up and down the aisles holding high either one finger urging a "yes" vote or two fingers urging defeat. House members then push either "yes," "no," or "present" buttons on their desks, which publicly record their votes on a large electronic scoreboard that displays green, red, and white lights by each legislator's name. Throughout this entire procedure, the speaker of the house presides by recognizing members from the floor, ruling on points of order, and attending to other parliamentary issues.

AP/Wide World Photos

Representative Jim Keffer urges an "aye" vote on the floor of the Texas house of representatives.

The Floor of the Senate   The senate floor may resemble that of the house in one sense—usually only a few members are paying attention to the debate. In the senate, even debates on important bills are much shorter than they are in the house, primarily because of the all-important "two-thirds rule" that requires suspension of the rules of the senate in order to bring a bill to the floor out of order (its regular calendar sequence). As this is the usual procedure for the consideration of bills in the senate, agreement by the lieutenant governor (for recognition from the floor) and at least two-thirds of senators implies that the major compromises have already been reached before the legislation ever reaches the floor.

The senate's tradition of unlimited debate means that the *filibuster* can threaten bills in the Texas senate as it does in the U.S. Senate. In the Texas senate, however, senators may not yield the floor to other senators who also want to filibuster. Here, the floor is controlled by the lieutenant governor. In other words, one senator may filibuster only as long as he or she can endure, and then the vote is taken. The filibuster in the Texas senate is used either to attract public attention to a bill that is sure to pass or to delay legislation in the closing days of the brief session. The mere threat of a filibuster is actually more important, for it can be a positive legislative weapon, especially at the end of the session when the supporters of the specific legislation may either withdraw their bill from intended consideration or modify it to reach a compromise with the disgruntled senator. A filibuster means that a compromise has become impossible, partly because a sufficient number of senators favors the bill so strongly that they are unmoved by the threat of a filibuster.

Following the debate, the senate vote is taken—without the benefit of an electronic scoreboard. Senators hold a single finger upward to indicate a "yes" vote or two fingers to vote "no." The vote is recorded by a clerk and only a simple majority is necessary to pass a bill.

The Conference Committee   A by-product of bicameralism is the necessity of resolving differences in similar bills that have passed both houses. The presiding officers appoint a conference committee to resolve differences between house and senate versions of a bill. Conference committees remain in contact with interested legislators and the presiding officers.

In Texas, conference committees are composed of five members from each house, appointed by their respective presiding officers. The compromise proposal must win the support of a majority of the committee members from each house if it is to be reported out of the conference committee. Because the members of the committee may either strengthen, weaken, or kill a bill, their attitudes are crucial to the various interests involved. This affords the presiding officers and conference committee members enviable bargaining positions. Bargaining is common both prior to the selection of the committee and during deliberations.

After a bill has been reported out of the conference committee, it may not be amended by either house, but must be accepted as written, rejected as written, or sent back to the conference committee for further compromise. In practice, because of the volume of legislation that must be considered in the limited time allotted, the Texas legislature tends to accept conference committee reports on most legislation.

HOW A BILL BECOMES A LAW IN TEXAS

Bills may be introduced into either house or, to speed the legislative process, into both houses at the same time. For purposes of simplicity, the following example will involve a bill that is introduced first into the senate before it is sent to the house.

The Senate

Although the initial idea for much legislation comes from special-interest groups, bureaucratic agencies, or powerful constituents, only members of the legislature may actually introduce bills. No bill, except for the general appropriations bill, may contain more than one subject, and this subject must be stated in the "caption," or title, of the bill. The bill will then be numbered and sent to the printer.

Legislators are often inattentive to formal debate and decisions are more likely to be made in smaller intimate negotiations among legislators. Here, presiding officer, Lieutenant Governor David Dewhirst negotiates with senators.

First Reading and Assignment to Committee   The constitution requires that bills be read to each house three times, on three separate days, a procedure that can be (and often is in the senate) suspended by a four-fifths vote. The first of these readings occurs when the senate secretary reads the caption of the bill to the senate and announces the committee to which it has been assigned by the lieutenant governor. If it is to have much chance of adoption, it is very important that the lieutenant governor choose a committee that does not oppose the spirit of the bill.

Committee Action   Committees are often called "little legislatures" because of the power they have over bills in their jurisdiction. The usual procedure is for the bill to be sent first to a subcommittee if one exists specializing in the bill's subject matter. Often bills are "pigeonholed" at this point and no further action is taken. If the bill has meaningful support, public hearings are held and the supporters and the opponents (usually lobbyists) are able to testify. Based on what they have learned and their own political considerations, subcommittee members "mark up," or rewrite the bill. The altered bill is then reported back to the committee, where it may be further modified. The committee may then report the bill favorably or unfavorably, or refuse to report it at all.

Second and Third Readings: Floor Action in the Senate   Once the bill is approved by the committee, its supporters are ready to move for tentative approval (second reading) and then final passage (third reading) by the full senate. To do this, the sponsor (the senator who first introduced the bill) must file a "notice of intent" to bring it up for debate on the following legislative day. The senator must also arrange for recognition on the floor by the lieutenant governor. If two-thirds of the senators agree to the senator's motion, the bill is ready for debate.

The president of the senate (the lieutenant governor) has the power to recognize senators who wish to speak, and to interpret rules and points of order. Amendments to the bill may be offered by any senator and a majority vote is needed to pass them.

Unlimited debate is the rule in the Texas senate. This does not imply that the senate is a deliberative body, for it is not; such luxury is precluded by the limited legislative session. Unlimited debate could, however, lead to a filibuster against a bill—literally an attempt to "talk the bill to death." Usually, however, if a bill reaches the floor of the senate, it has already cleared the major obstacle (the two-thirds majority necessary for senate consideration) and will be passed in some form. Following a vote in which only a simple majority is necessary, the bill is passed to its third reading. Third reading and final passage are usually routine matters for bills that have made it this far through the senate. Debate may again take place, and amendments may again be offered on third reading, but a two-thirds vote is now needed to pass proposed amendments. Final passage of the bill itself requires a simple majority vote.

The House

Following senate passage, the bill is sent to the house of representatives. A procedure similar to that used in the senate is followed again in the house.

First Reading and Assignment to Committee   The bill must also be read on three separate days in the house. The first of these readings occurs when the clerk reads the caption of the bill and announces the committee to which it has been assigned. The speaker of the house assigns bills to the various committees and he or she, like the lieutenant governor, has considerable freedom of choice because the jurisdiction of house committees over specific kinds of legislation is somewhat vague.

Committee Action   Committee action in the house is similar to that taken in the senate. The bill is assigned to a committee, and then to a subcommittee, which may hold public hearings. The subcommittee, as well as the committee itself, may amend, totally rewrite, or pigeonhole the bill.

The Committee on Calendars   A bill that is reported favorably by committee, or that receives a favorable minority report by the required number of committee members, is placed on one of the house legislative calendars by the Committee on Calendars. This establishes the approximate order in which the legislation will be considered by the whole house. If the Committee on Calendars fails to assign the bill to a calendar, it may be forced to do so by the action of a simple majority of the house.

Second and Third Readings: Floor Action in the House   As in the senate, the bill must be tentatively approved (second reading) and then finally passed (third reading) by the full house. The speaker of the house has the power to recognize representatives on the house floor and to interpret the rules and points of order.

The size of the house necessitates that debate be more limited than in the senate—usually to ten minutes for each member. Bills may be amended, defeated, tabled, sent back to committee, or passed by a simple majority of those members present.

Third reading and final passage of legislation in the house is, as it was in the senate, a fairly routine matter for bills that have survived the prior legislative process. Amendments may be offered at this time, but a two-thirds vote is needed for their adoption. A simple majority vote is needed for a bill's final passage.

The Conference Committee

If the house has made a change in the senate version of the bill, a conference committee is necessary to iron out the differences between the two houses' versions. The lieutenant governor appoints five senators and the speaker appoints five representatives to sit on the committee. The compromise bill must receive a majority of both the senate and the house members before it can be reported out of the conference committee.

Final Passage

If the change is a minor one, there is no difficulty with the compromise; the bill is reported back to the senate and house for action. Neither the senate nor the house can amend the reported bill; both must accept it, reject it, or send it back to the conference committee. The conference committee's compromise version of this bill, backed by its supporters, is approved by both houses and sent to the governor for his or her action.

The Governor

A governor has several alternatives once the bill reaches his or her desk. Within ten days during the session or twenty days after adjournment, the governor may sign or ignore the bill and it will then become law. The Texas governor does not have a "pocket veto"—ignoring a bill after adjournment does not kill a bill in Texas. To kill a bill during the session the governor must send it back to the house of origin with a veto message explaining his or her objections. After adjournment, the governor files veto messages with the secretary of state. The legislature may override the veto by a two-thirds vote in each house. With most bills, the governor must either accept or reject the total bill; only with appropriations bills can he or she veto specific items within the bill—the line-item veto. When the governor receives a bill late enough in the legislative session, he or she can wait until the legislature adjourns to veto the bill without fear of a legislative override; after-session vetoes are always final. If the governor signs the bill, it takes effect in ninety days (except for appropriations and those bills the legislature has designated as emergency legislation). Figure 5.5 illustrates how a bill becomes a law in Texas.

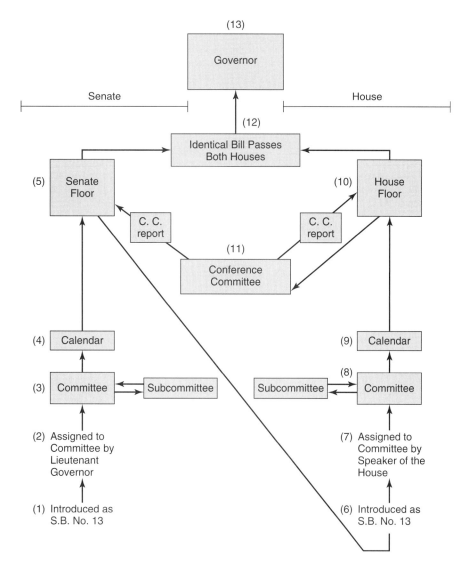

FIGURE 5.5 How a Bill Becomes a Law in Texas

NONPROCEDURAL TOOLS OF LEADERSHIP

When the legislature begins its appropriations process to determine funding levels for the next two-year period, it traditionally starts by using a budget prepared and submitted by the Legislative Budget Board. All state agencies are required to submit their budget requests to this board (and also to the governor's budget office), which then analyzes them and prepares a suggested budget.

The Legislative Budget Board is a joint senate-house committee that operates continuously, even when the legislature is not in session. It is made up of ten members, including the lieutenant governor and speaker (who serve as joint chairs), and four members from each house, who are appointed by their respective presiding officers. Members include the chairs of the senate Finance committee and the house Appropriations and Ways and Means committees.

Clearly, control of the board is in the hands of the two presiding officers, who are in a position to strongly influence, if not control, state spending from the budgeting stage through the final appropriating stage. The staff under their control, which assists the appropriating committees and their chairs, also serves a watchdog function, overseeing to some extent the expenditures of the executive agencies and departments. Thus, in this critical area of finance, the concentration of power in the presiding officers is even greater than in other areas.

The Legislative Council

Another instrument of leadership is the fourteen-member Legislative Council. The lieutenant governor and speaker serve as joint chairpersons, and six members from the house and six from the senate are appointed by their respective presiding officers. The administrative work of the council is done by a director and professional staff, who serve at the pleasure of the council.

The in-session function of the council is to provide bill-drafting services for the legislators. Between sessions, the council staff researches subjects to be considered in the next legislative session and provides staff for interim committees that might be appointed to study a specific subject or problem assigned to them.

The Legislative Audit Committee

The Legislative Audit Committee is composed of six members, including the presiding officers and the chairs of four standing committees (the house Ways and Means and Appropriations committees and the senate Finance and State Affairs committees) appointed by the presiding officers. The audit committee supervises the state auditor and staff that officially review in detail all state agency and departmental expenditures.

The Sunset Advisory Commission

The Sunset Advisory Commission is composed of twelve members, including legislators and public citizens appointed by the speaker and lieutenant governor. Every two years the commission elects a chair from among its members, alternating the position between the house and the senate. This committee reevaluates twenty to thirty state agencies every two years, and each state agency undergoes review at least every twelve years to determine if there is a need for its existence. This is a powerful commission because it may recommend killing an agency or dramatically changing its function.

RESTRAINTS ON THE POWERS
OF THE PRESIDING OFFICERS

Although the whole of these organizational, procedural, and nonprocedural powers seems to be and at times is overwhelming, certain restraints curtail the arbitrary and absolute use of these powers by the speaker and the lieutenant governor.

Personality

The personalities of the individual presiding officers, and the way they view their offices, determine their approach to legislative leadership. They may use their powers to develop aggressive leadership, ruthlessly overpowering opposition, or they may be accommodating and compromising, accomplishing their desired results through only the implied threat of reprisal.

The Team

It is easy to oversimplify the concentration of power enjoyed by the presiding officers, who could not exercise their power without a strong consensus among Republicans and occasionally a few conservative Democrats. This coalition results from personal friendship and primarily from shared political goals. Generally, legislators feel that it is in the best interests of their constituents and supporters to be "team players" and back the presiding officers. The speaker and the lieutenant governor are usually able to build support through their powers to reward or punish.

Although there is no absolute control of the "team," its members usually cooperate closely with their presiding officers. In the final analysis, those who "go along" with the presiding officers "get along." At times, the presiding officers and their "teams" take no position on a bill, and then legislators are able to vote according to their consciences or the interests of their own supporters without fear of reprisal.

The Lobby and Bureaucrats

The relationship between the presiding officers and the lobby (with its bureaucratic allies) often determines the chance of success for specific legislation. When the lieutenant governor, speaker, bureaucrats, and lobbyists all work together toward a common goal, legislative victory is almost assured.

In the event of conflict between the lobby-bureaucratic coalition and the speaker and lieutenant governor, the program of the presiding officers may be either diluted or defeated, depending on such complex factors as the level of gubernatorial, interest-group, and legislative support the presiding officers can muster. Against a strong interest group-bureaucratic coalition, the presiding officers, even with all their formal and informal powers, would find it difficult to control legislation. They simply would be confronted by too much combined political power. The chance of such a conflict is remote, for more often than not, the presiding officers are in basic agreement with the more powerful interests, which have often provided them with political and financial support.

The Governor

Among the most important powers given the governor in the Texas Constitution are those that concern legislation. They include the power to call special sessions, the veto, and the line-item veto over appropriations—formal powers that place the governor in a strong bargaining position. Apart from his or her clout with the lobby, the veto threat is the governor's most useful instrument to influence changes in a bill while it is still in the legislature.

Often, the interest groups that supported the governor have also supported the lieutenant governor and the speaker, and the governor often encourages these interest groups to exert influence on the presiding officers and other legislators. If the governor tends toward legislative activism, he or she can exercise considerable influence over legislation in spite of the powers of the presiding officers. If the governor chooses a passive legislative role, the powers of the presiding officers are subsequently increased. Inaction or restraint affects public policy as deeply as an activist leadership.

The Political Climate

The general public is seldom aware of events in Austin, although there are rare exceptions—such as when there exists a climate of corruption, like the veterans' land scandals of the 1950s or the Sharpstown Bank scandal of the 1970s. At such times, the public is more concerned with a search for "whipping boys" than with concerted inquiry into basic government procedures and an insistence on meaningful reform that could reduce the likelihood of similar scandals. A crisis situation such as the school-finance issue has been brewing since the 1980s, but the general public has only recently become acutely aware of the problem. At least for a while, the public will be attentive, and the presiding officers will be aware of public scrutiny.

Otherwise, interest groups, administrators, a few concerned citizens, and the governor are generally the only ones who exhibit a continuing interest in the activity in the Texas legislature.

Political or Economic Ambition

Through effective management of the press, accumulation of political credits to be collected at some future date, and consolidation of interest-group support, the speaker and lieutenant governor can use their offices as excellent stepping-stones for advancement in their political or financial ambitions. The presiding officers must not, however, antagonize powerful economic and political forces. The presiding officers must play their political cards carefully in order to build an economic and political base solid enough to attain higher office. The lieutenant governor, speaker, and governor often compete for power.

Other Legislators

Many committee chairs and individual legislators exercise a great deal of power in their own right, through their mastery of the intricacies of legislative rules and procedures, and the respect (or fear) that they have generated in other legislators. Because of the ties that these individuals have established with administrators, strong interest groups, and other legislators, the presiding officers may need to solicit their support on key legislation.

CONCLUSION

The Texas legislature is similar in many respects to the U.S. Congress and most state legislatures. They are bicameral and both houses pass a law following the same basic steps—introduction, committee consideration, scheduling, and floor action. After a conference committee compromises house and senate versions, a bill is passed by majority vote of each house and is sent to the executive to be signed, vetoed, or allowed to become law without the governor's signature.

In addition to low salaries, biennial sessions, and limited staff support, the Texas legislature also differs from the U.S. Congress and many state legislatures in several respects. Rather than diffusing power among party leaders and caucuses, Texas concentrates power in the hands of the presiding officers, the speaker of the house and the lieutenant governor in the senate. Such centralization makes it possible for the legislature to function in brief, infrequent sessions. The presiding officers have become the instruments of the majority Republican party.

The dominance of the presiding officers is not entirely arbitrary. The speaker of the house is elected by a majority of its members, and the majority in each house of the legislature adopts the rules that give presiding officers most of their power. The lieutenant governor, elected for a four-year term by Texas voters, must maintain some appearance of bipartisanship because of the two-thirds rule for scheduling legislation and the threat of filibusters.

In few, if any, states is the legislature so important and, in none are its presiding officers so important as in Texas.

KEY TERMS

bicameral	gerrymandering	pigeonholing
biennial session	item veto	speaker of the house
calendar	Legislative Budget Board	special session
conference committees	lieutenant governor	standing committee chair
filibuster	lobbyist	standing committees
floor action	mark-up	veto

Logging On

The Texas Legislature Online has much information on the Texas legislature at **http://www.capitol.state.tx.us/**. Click on legislative process in the left for an excellent explanation of procedure. An interesting feature of this site is Who Represents Me? Click on this link and it will take you to the Find Your Incumbent (FYI) page. Follow the instructions, and it allows you to find your state senator and representative.

One of the most improved sites is the Legislative Reference Library at **www.lrb.state.tx.us**. Check the status of bills, the history of legislative sessions, and an explanation of proposed constitutional amendments and bill analysis.

The Legislative Budget Board, which helps the legislature prepare the budget, is located at **http://www.lbb.state.tx.us/**.

The Texas Legislative Council (TLC) has the new legislative districts. Go to **www.tlc.state.tx.us**. Click on site index and go to redistricting services.

ENDNOTES

1. *Reynolds v. Sims*, 377 U.S. 533 (1968).
2. *Wesberry v. Sanders*, 376 U.S. 1 (1964).

6

The Executive

INTRODUCTION

THE GOVERNOR AND THE OFFICE

The executive branch of Texas government is divided into numerous elective and appointive offices, primarily because Texans traditionally fear concentration of power anywhere in government, but particularly in the executive branch. This fear is compounded by legislators' reluctance to pass laws that would increase the powers of the chief executive relative to their own. As a result, the Texas executive branch has evolved into a hodgepodge of elective offices, boards, and commissions, all separate from and largely independent of the governor. In spite of these constitutional and statutory restrictions, however, the governor can influence state policy by persuading and bargaining with others.

Formal Qualifications

The legal requirements for the office are minimal. The governor must be thirty years old and an American citizen, and have lived in Texas for five years prior to the election.

Republican Governor Rick Perry shares much power with fellow Republicans Lt. Gov. David Dewhurst (right) and Tom Craddick (left).

Informal Qualifications

Although millions of Texans satisfy these formal qualifications, informal qualifications more strictly limit the number of possible contenders. The typical governor has been Anglo-Saxon, Protestant, male, middle-aged, a family person, and a businessperson or attorney. In 1990 Texans elected Governor Ann Richards, the only woman to hold the office since Miriam A. Ferguson was elected in 1924 and 1932. Most Texas governors historically were conservative Democrats, but voters now usually elect Republicans to statewide offices. Republicans (including Governor Rick Perry) have held the governorship four out of the last six terms.

Terms and Tenure

The governor is elected for a four-year term. There is no limit on the number of terms a Texas governor may serve. Table 6.1 compares the terms and qualifications of elected chief executives in the United States.

The governor (and other elected and appointed executives) may be removed from office only by a process of impeachment and conviction. Impeachment (equivalent to indictment) requires a majority vote of those present in the house of representatives. An impeached governor then may be convicted by two-thirds of the members present in the senate. If that happens, the governor is removed

T A B L E 6.1 Terms and Qualifications of Elected Chief Executives

Constitutional Provisions	Texas Governor	U.S. President	The Fifty States' Governors
Age	30 years	35 years	34 states set minimum age at 30
Residence	5 years	14 years	5 years or less in 38 states
Terms	4 years	4 years (limited to 2 terms or 10 years)	48 states allow a 4-year term, but, unlike Texas, 36 states limit number of consecutive terms.

SOURCE: Council of State Governments, *Book of the States 2005* (Lexington, KY: 2005), pp. 215–7.

and barred from any other public office. In the event the governor's office becomes vacant, whether through impeachment and conviction, death, or resignation, the successor is the lieutenant governor.

Compensation

At present, the governor's salary is set by statute at $115,345 yearly. In contrast to the very low salaries paid to Texas legislators, the governor's salary ranks among the highest in the United States. Additional benefits include the governor's mansion, an expense account to keep it maintained, and a professional staff with offices in the capitol.

Staff

The complexity of modern government requires that a governor depend heavily on staff personnel to assist in everyday duties of the office and to coordinate efforts to persuade legislators, administrators, and local officials to follow the governor's leadership. The staff also assists in state planning and evaluates potential gubernatorial appointees. Thus, the governor depends on others for advice, information, and assistance. An efficient, loyal staff is a key ingredient in the successful tenure of any Texas chief executive.

Tools of Persuasion

A governor's ability to influence the making and execution of public policy depends on a combination of formal and informal powers. Formal powers are those granted to the governor by either the state constitution or statutes. For example, the Texas constitution grants the governor the power to veto legislation or to call special legislative sessions and set their agendas. However, the governor may not order reorganization of the executive branch and must share budgetary power with the influential Legislative Budget Board. The governor must also share executive power with several independently elected officers and boards in a plural executive system. Figure 6.1 compares important constitutional powers of the fifty governors and indicates that the Texas governor is among the weakest.

FIGURE 6.1 Constitutional Powers of the Governors

The constitutional powers considered were full-budget responsibility, item veto on appropriations, reorganization by executive order, and sharing power with fewer than seven executive officials elected statewide independently from the governor.
SOURCE: Data from *The Book of the States 2002,* pp. 150–51, Council of State Governments.

Statutes provide the governor with some formal powers such as appointing members of the boards and commissions that supervise most state agencies. However, members are appointed for six-year overlapping terms so that governors must wait several years for terms to expire before being able to fill vacancies with their appointees. These boards, in turn, appoint their respective agencies' chief administrators, who answer to the boards and not to the governor.

Despite these restrictions on their formal powers, some Texas governors have been able to wield effective power because of their personalities, public relations, the political and economic climate, and the political strength of their supporters. Governors Allan Shivers, John Connally, and George W. Bush relied on these informal powers along with their formal powers to develop more influence than most Texas governors.

Legislative Tools   Ironically, Texas governors' most effective bargaining tools are legislative. How they use these tools determines to a large extent their effectiveness in the overall governing process.

The Veto   One of the most powerful formal legislative tools at the governor's disposal is the veto. After a bill has passed both houses of the legislature in identical form, it is sent to the governor's desk. If the governor signs it, the bill becomes law; but if the governor vetoes it, the bill goes back to the legislature with a message stating the reasons for opposition. The legislature has the constitutional power to override the governor's veto by a two-thirds vote, but in practice vetoes are usually final. As legislative sessions in Texas are short, the vast majority of important bills are passed and sent to the governor within the final ten days of the legislative session. Because the governor need take no action on the legislation for ten days when the legislature is in session (twenty days when it is not in session), he or she can wait until the legislature has adjourned and thus ensure that a veto cannot be overridden.

The Texas governor lacks pocket veto power (the power to kill a bill by ignoring it after the legislature has adjourned). In the event that the governor neither signs nor vetoes a bill, it becomes law without a signature. By not signing a bill but allowing it to become law, the governor registers a symbolic protest against the bill or some of its sections.

The Item Veto   Probably the single most important piece of legislation enacted in a legislative session is the appropriations bill. In fact, so important is this bill, that if the governor were to veto it in its entirety after the legislature had adjourned, there would be no funds for the operation of the Texas government, and a special session of the legislature would be necessary. Thus, the veto of an entire appropriations bill is usually impractical, and Texas, along with 42 other states, permits an item veto, which allows the governor to strike funds for specific projects or programs from appropriations bills. Used to its fullest potential, the item veto is very effective as a negative legislative weapon. As the appropriations bill is usually passed at the very end of the legislative session, the item veto is usually exercised after adjournment and the legislature has no opportunity to override it.

The Threat to Veto   As an informal legislative power of the governor, the threat to veto is not mentioned in the constitution or the law. Nevertheless, it is a very real and effective tool for the governor. Like all informal powers, its effectiveness depends on existing formal powers.

LEGISLATORS   Both the veto and the item veto are negative tools that simply kill bills or items of appropriation; they do not in themselves help the governor shape legislation. However, by threatening to use these formal powers, the governor can often persuade the supporters of a bill to change its contents. In this way, an apt compromise can often be negotiated between the governor and the bill's supporters. Thus, while the veto itself is negative, the "threat to veto" can be used to shape legislation in a positive way.

ADMINISTRATORS   *Administrators,* both elective and appointive, are active in the legislative process and seek increased funding for favorite programs or projects, as well as authorization to administer new programs. The governor may be able to influence the administration of existing programs by threatening to veto appropriations or other bills actively supported by an agency. The agency's legislative liaison personnel (that is, the agency's lobbyists) may also be encouraged to support the governor's legislative program in exchange for his or her support of agency bills.

LOBBYISTS   The governor can often consolidate lobby support for his or her legislative proposals by threatening a veto. Lobbyists may offer to support the governor's position on legislation if he or she will agree not to veto a particular bill considered vital to their interests. The governor can thus bargain with both supporters and opponents of legislation and gain political allies.

Special Sessions   According to the Texas constitution, only the governor has the power to call the legislature into special session and to determine the subjects to be considered. Often, when coalitions of legislators and lobbyists request the governor to call a special session so that a critical issue concerning state government can be brought before the legislature, other coalitions of legislators and interests are opposed to the special session. The opponents may feel either that the issue is not critical and that its enactment would cost the state too much money, or that their particular economic or political interest would suffer.

As there is seldom any important legislation passed that does not hurt some and help others, the special session can be a valuable bargaining tool for the governor. For example, he or she may refuse to call a special session in return for support from the opposition at some future date, or may call a special session but refuse to include a subject for consideration until its supporters meet his or her terms. The opponents may, of course, outbid the supporters, and the topic may never be considered. If the governor has strong feelings about the proposal and is determined either to call or not to call a special session, the issue may not be open to negotiation.

Message Power   The governor is constitutionally required to deliver a message at the beginning of the legislative session. In this State of the State message, the governor outlines his or her legislative agenda. From time to time throughout the session, the governor may also submit messages calling for other legislative action.

The governor's message power is a formal power, which is enhanced by the visibility of the office. Through the judicious use of the mass media (an informal power), the governor can focus immediate public attention on a bill that might otherwise be buried in the complicated legislative maze. Access to publicity enabled former Governor George W. Bush to use his state office as a springboard to the presidency.

Executive Tools of Persuasion   The constitution names the governor as the chief executive responsible for the faithful execution of the laws, but it also systematically establishes a framework that makes it impossible to carry out this broad goal. It creates a plural executive system by establishing several other independently elected executive officers with whom the governor must share power. The lieutenant governor, comptroller of public accounts, commissioner of the General Land Office, and attorney general are elected for four year terms. The constitution establishes a fifteen-member State Board of Education to be elected or appointed and a three-member Railroad Commission elected for six-year staggered terms.

Historically, the legislature has, by statute, assumed executive functions such as budgeting and auditing, and created a multitude of independent boards and commissions. The legislature has also created an elected commissioner of agriculture and provided that the Board of Education shall be elected. The result is a further fragmenting of executive power. Sensing long-term Republican control of both the legislative and executive branches, the legislature is only beginning to consider efforts to increase the governor's executive power.

Given the fragmented nature of the executive branch, the governor still has fewer tools to bargain with administrative agencies than most states' governors. In fact, the legislature asserts considerable control over state agencies because it creates most of those agencies, gives them their power, appropriates their funds, and investigates their activities.

Appointive Powers　Appointment is probably the governor's most important executive power, and an effective governor must use it wisely. The most important appointments the governor makes are those to the independent boards and commissions. Members of these boards establish general policy for the agency or institution under their jurisdiction, and they usually choose the administrators who carry out these policies and administer and interpret the law.

The governor has some bargaining power with concerned interest groups (clientele groups) involving the appointments made to these boards. It is vital to these interest groups that the "right kind" of appointees be selected. Industries are particularly interested in having a business advocate appointed to the board that oversees and sets policy affecting their enterprises. A consumer advocate could, to some extent, disrupt the close working relationship that usually exists between the industry and the agency. There may also be competing interest groups within one industry. These competing groups may bargain individually with the governor in an attempt to place an appointee on the board who supports their particular viewpoint.

Removal Powers　Although the governor appoints numerous members of boards and commissions, he or she has very limited removal powers. The governor may remove only those officers he or she has appointed, and, except for staff members, two-thirds of the senate must also approve the firing. In practice, the governor has limited powers to issue directives or orders to state agencies, and cannot remove executive officials because of their disloyalty or failure to support his or her proposals. However, by focusing public attention on an errant agency, the governor may be able to force its administrator to change policy or resign.

Planning Powers　The governor has become the central figure in interagency planning and the coordination of regional and local planning with affected state agencies; he or she also helps coordinate the planning of local governments and regional organizations. This recent increase in planning functions has added to the governor's overall importance and prestige, but it is not a particularly firm

© Joel Salcido/Daemmrich Associate

Ceremonial events are part of the governor's role as chief of state.

foundation for political bargaining. Again, the governor has been granted responsibility without the enforcement powers necessary to carry it out (he or she has no power to enforce compliance from the various state agencies and local governments).

What power the governor does have in this area is largely derived from the policies of the national government. In the past, there was little coordination between the policies and programs of the various local governments and those of the state government. As a condition for receiving federal grants, Texas was required to develop some kind of overall procedure for program development. The natural hub for any statewide planning was the governor's office, which has now been used as a focal point to determine whether grant requests are in accord with statewide plans.

Chief of State   The governor, as the First Citizen of Texas, serves as a symbol of Texas. Given the visibility of the office, its occupant is able to focus the public's attention on legislative proposals, state problems, and other administrators as can no other state official.

A major part of the governor's job is related to the pomp and ceremony of the office. Relevant duties include greeting Boy Scout troops at the state capitol, visiting disaster areas, entertaining officials of other governments, and riding in parades for peanut festivals, city centennials, and cow-chip-throwing contests. Used properly, the ceremonial duties of the office, though tiresome and time-consuming, can accent the governor's prestige and increase his or her influence with other politicians and administrators in the state government.

The governor is also responsible for coordinating Texas's relations with other states. He or she serves as a member of (or appoints representatives to) numerous multi-state organizations and conferences. The governor also requests assistance from the national government following natural disasters, droughts, or economic calamities. The request for aid is made publicly, both to solidify public opinion behind the request and to get Washington officials to use their influence to procure as much assistance as quickly as possible. All these roles serve to provide the governor with increased leadership potential.

Budget Powers   The governor is officially the chief budget officer of the state. Each biennium, the various agencies and institutions submit their funding requests, to be incorporated into the governor's budget. Working from these estimates, the governor's staff prepares a budget based both on the state's estimated income and the estimated cost of the program proposals. When completed, the budget is submitted to the legislature, which promptly disregards most of the governor's budget and concentrates instead on the budget proposals prepared by the Legislative Budget Board.

Law Enforcement Powers   The governor has very little law enforcement power. Following the basic pattern of Texas government, law enforcement is decentralized. State judges are elected, and criminal acts are prosecuted either by elected district and county attorneys or by appointed city attorneys. The police are equally decentralized. At the state level, enforcement is conducted by the Texas Highway Patrol or the Texas Rangers. Both organizations are under the command of the Department of Public Safety and its director, who is appointed by an independent board, the Public Safety Commission. Only in the event of riots or disasters can the governor assume control over the Texas Department of Public Safety. He or she has no direct authority over other law enforcement officials. Local police operate under the jurisdiction of county sheriffs and constables (who are elected) and city chiefs of police (appointed by city officials).

Military Powers   The governor is commander-in-chief of the state militia, which consists of two basic parts: the Texas National Guard and the Texas State Guard. The governor appoints the adjutant general to command these units and may order them to keep the peace and protect public property following riots or national disasters. He or she may also employ the militia to "suppress insurrection, repel invasions, and protect the frontier from hostile incursions by Indians" or other lawless bands. This power has not been used in recent years.

The Texas National Guard, consisting of both army and air force components, is financed by the national government. It is required to meet federal standards and may be called to active duty by the president. In the event the guard is mobilized, command passes from the governor to the president.

Clemency Powers   The governor may grant clemency, but only on the recommendation of the Board of Pardons and Paroles (made up of seven board members and eleven commissioners). Although the governor may not grant more clemency than the board recommends, he or she may grant less. The governor may independently grant a thirty-day postponement of execution without the board's recommendation.

THE TEXAS BUREAUCRACY

Although the governor is designated by the constitution as the chief executive, it is really the other administrators (bureaucrats) who see that the laws are properly administered. The law is administered when a highway is built, when a police officer writes a ticket, when taxes are collected, or when a public school teacher conducts a class. Public administrators check gas pumps and meat scales for accuracy; license barbers, doctors, and morticians; regulate insurance policies; and arrest poachers for illegal hunting.

The most distinctive characteristic of the Texas administration is that no single person is really in charge of the administrative apparatus. As in many other states, the administrative structure in Texas is split among several appointed or elected executives and numerous boards and commissions.

No single official in the Texas government bears the ultimate responsibility for the actions of the Texas bureaucracy. There is no single official who can coordinate either planning or program implementation among the many agencies, commissions, and departments. The Texas bureaucracy can be visualized as about 200 separate entities, each following its own course, often oblivious of the plans and programs of other agencies. Cooperation among agencies with respect to the effects of their policy decisions on each others' programs is slight.

Although the structure of the executive branch of government is both complex and diverse, administrative organizations can be classified according to the method used to select their top policymakers, as follows:

1. Single elected administrators
2. Appointed executives
3. Boards and commissions, including elected, *ex officio,* and appointed boards.

Single Elected Administrators

Like the governor, major Texas elected executives are elected for four-year terms, with no limit on the number of terms they may serve. The election of several administrators (in addition to the governor) was intended to decentralize administrative power and prevent any one individual from gaining complete control of the government. The elected officials are to be held responsible to the people for their administrative competence, as well as for their political positions, but few Texans can name the individuals in these offices, much less judge their relative competence.

The Lieutenant Governor Although the lieutenant governor is technically a part of the executive branch, his or her duties are in fact almost entirely legislative. The lieutenant governor's most important powers are as presiding officer over the state senate. His or her administrative responsibilities are confined to serving *ex officio* (by virtue of the office) on a few boards and appointing members to some boards and commissions.

The Attorney General Considered one of the most powerful officers in Texas government, the attorney general is the lawyer for all the officials, boards, and agencies in state government. The office also deals with everything from antitrust actions and consumer protection to activities concerning insurance, banking, and securities. A broad spectrum of the state's business—oil and gas, law enforcement, environmental protection, highways, transportation, and charitable trusts, to name only a few—is included in the jurisdiction of the attorney general.

Lt. Governor Dewhurst (Rep.)

The attorney general's responsibilities include

1. Giving legal advice to state officials, boards, agencies, or legislators concerning the legality or constitutionality of administrative actions, laws, or proposed laws. State officials usually follow the attorney general's advice because the attorney general's office will not defend in court officials who do not follow attorney general opinions. The attorney general's opinions are often the most authoritative interpretations available on many legal issues. The attorney general's interpretations are not usually challenged in the courts.

2. Representing the state in civil litigation. This includes conflicts with the national government and the governments of other states. Suits against corporations, such as antitrust litigation for consumer protection, also are initiated by the attorney general.

Attorney General Abbott (Rep.)

Comptroller of Public Accounts The comptroller is both the chief tax administrator and the chief preaudit accounting officer in the Texas government. Among other duties, he or she is required by the constitution to certify the approximate biennial income for the state. The comptroller's estimates are binding because the constitution requires a four-fifths vote for the state legislature to appropriate more funds than are anticipated as income for any biennial session. Only state constitutional amendments can authorize the issuance of bonds to finance borrowing.

Commissioner of the General Land Office The principal duties of the commissioner are to

1. Supervise leasing activities on Texas public lands
2. Approve leases for oil and minerals on the subsurface property owned by the state
3. Administer the veterans' land program, under which veterans can borrow money to buy land using bonds authorized by Texas voters

Comptroller of Public Accounts Carole Keeton Rylander (Rep.)

As is the case with many officials, the land commissioner serves as an ex officio member or chair of several important boards, including the Veterans' Land Board.

Commissioner of Agriculture   The commissioner of agriculture is responsible for administering laws relating to agriculture, as well as other research, educational, and regulatory activities. The duties of the department range from checking scales in meat markets and gas pumps in service stations to determining labeling procedures for pesticides and promoting Texas agricultural products in the national and world markets.

Like the U.S. Department of Agriculture, the Texas department is charged with administration of laws both for consumer protection and for the agribusiness industry. A conflict of interest between these two groups is very likely; in such a conflict, the primary constituent group (agribusiness interests) is usually given priority.

Appointed Administrators

Secretary of State   The governor appoints the secretary of state to serve as the state's chief record keeper and elections officer. He or she enforces uniform interpretation and application of the election laws, distributes election supplies, and receives election results. The secretary of state acts in the capacity of notary, attesting to the signature of the governor on various documents, charters corporations, licenses public notaries, routinely processes extradition documents, and holds hearings concerning the extradition of reluctant fugitives.

Adjutant General   Appointed by the governor and confirmed by the senate for a two-year term, the adjutant general is the state's top-ranking military officer, who exercises administrative jurisdiction over the Texas National Guard and the Texas State Guard. It is one of the few state agencies under the direct administrative control of the governor.

Insurance Commissioner   The Texas Department of Insurance is headed by a commissioner appointed directly by the governor for a two-year fixed term, subject to senate confirmation. The department monitors and regulates the Texas insurance industry. It provides consumer information, monitors corporate solvency, prosecutes violators of insurance law, licenses agents and investigates complaints against them, develops statistics for rate determination, and regulates specific insurance lines such as property, liability, and life.

Boards and Commissions

A major portion of Texas law is administered by boards and commissions that establish general policy and appoint executive directors responsible for the day-to-day operations of the agency. These executives are responsible for budgeting and for administering state and federal laws and directives, as well as for implementing board policy.

Elective Boards   Voters elect two multimember boards, both of which are of major importance in Texas's bureaucracy.

The Texas Railroad Commission   Texas's most important regulatory body is the Railroad Commission, an elective board whose three members serve for overlapping six-year terms. The governor fills vacancies on the board, and appointees serve until the next election.

The board is politically partisan, and its members must first win nomination in their party's primary before they are elected in the general election. The incumbent who is next up for reelection serves as the chair for the two years prior to the election. The duties of the commission include regulation of gas utilities, oil and gas pipelines, and pumping activities. It is also responsible for regulation of waste disposal by the oil and gas industry, and for the protection of both surface and subsurface water supplies from oil- or gas-related residue. In their election campaigns, successful Railroad Commission candidates usually have the endorsement of much of the oil and gas industry, and they have been responsive to the industries they regulate.

State Board of Education   The State Board of Education (SBE) is elected in partisan elections for four-year staggered terms from fifteen single-member districts. The governor appoints the chair from the SBE membership for a two-year term. The SBE establishes policy, implements policy established by law, and oversees the Texas Education Agency (TEA). The board also recommends three nominees for commissioner of education (the TEA's chief executive officer), from whom the commissioner is appointed by the governor, with the senate's consent, to a four-year term.

Texas has historically had a decentralized public-school system, in which most educational and administrative policy is established by local school boards. Recently, however, more and more educational policy is being mandated by the legislature, the courts, and the TEA. The TEA writes regulations for and compels local compliance with legislative and judicial mandates and reforms, dispenses state funds, serves as a conduit for some funds from the national government to the local schools, and selects the textbooks to be purchased at state expense for use by local districts.

Ex Officio Boards   For several reasons, numerous boards are filled either partially or totally with ex officio members who also hold other offices. When travel to Austin was both expensive and time-consuming (before the advent of the superhighway), the logical course of action for a state committed to the board-and-commission system of administration was to establish boards consisting of officials who were already in Austin. The following is one example of an ex officio board.

Legislative Redistricting Board   The Legislative Redistricting Board consists of five ex officio members: the lieutenant governor, the speaker of the house, the attorney general, the commissioner of the General Land Office, and the comptroller. The board is required to redraw the state senatorial and representative districts if the legislature fails to redistrict itself following the decennial census. When the divided legislature was unable to redraw districts after the 2000 census, the Republican-dominated board redrew districts that increased Republican representation from 48 to 59 percent.

Appointed Boards   The appointive boards vary considerably with respect to their importance, administrative power, and function. Members of these boards, who usually are nonsalaried, set the general agency policy and appoint their own chief administrator. Generally, board members are appointed by the governor, with the consent of the senate, but there are many mixed boards whose members are appointed by the governor or by some other official, or which have partially ex officio membership. There are about 200 boards or commissions in the Texas bureaucracy, including those that administer the following areas of public policy.

Administration of Colleges and Universities   The eighteen members of the Coordinating Board of the Texas College and University System are appointed by the governor with the consent of the senate and serve six-year staggered terms. The board appoints a commissioner of higher education, who supervises the board's staff. Together the board and commissioner plan for the future needs of higher education in the state in terms of programs, curricula, and facilities.

Although the coordinating board has the authority to determine the general role of each public college and university, these institutions are governed by boards of regents or trustees. These boards of regents (each consisting of nine members) are appointed by the governor with the consent of the senate, for six-year overlapping terms. Community colleges are governed by locally elected multimember boards of trustees. Within the limits of state law and the guidelines established by the coordinating board, the regents and trustees make basic policies for institutions under their jurisdictions.

Administration of Social Service Programs   Aside from public education, social services include the most costly state programs. The Commission of Health and Human Services serves as an umbrella, managing and directing four divisions.

1. Department of Aging and Disability Services
2. Department of State Health Services
3. Department of Assistive and Rehabilitative Services
4. Department of Family Protective Services

These departments provide Temporary Assistance for Needy Families (TANF), child welfare services, and the food-stamp program. Additionally, they serve the blind and mentally retarded. The health department attempts to control communicable diseases, operates tuberculosis hospitals and clinics, and keeps vital statistics on births, deaths, and the like.

The unemployment insurance program in Texas is administered separately by the Texas Workforce Commission (TWC), a board of five members appointed by the governor, with the consent of the senate, for six-year overlapping terms. The TWC administers benefit payments, job placement, and training and rehabilitation services for those seeking work.

Administration of Highway Programs   The state Department of Transportation (DOT), governed by a five-member Texas Transportation Commission, is primarily responsible for the state's several highway building and maintenance programs. DOT is also responsible for registering motor vehicles and assisting local communities in development of public transportation.

Regulation of Financial Institutions   Stocks and other securities sold in Texas may be subject to the regulation of the State Securities Board, a three-member board appointed by the governor for six-year overlapping terms. Like the Securities and Exchange Commission of the national government, the State Securities Board is charged with preventing the sale of worthless or fraudulent securities and other illegal stock dealings.

Licensing Boards   More than thirty examining boards license individuals who practice various trades and professions in Texas. Standards and qualifying examinations are usually a prerequisite to licensing; licenses may be revoked by the boards for either unethical conduct or nonpayment of fees. Examining and licensing boards are primarily supported by dues collected from the members of the licensed occupations. Examining and licensing boards include the State Board of Barber Examiners, the Court Reporters Certification Board, and the Texas State Board of Medical Examiners.

Other Boards and Commissions   At least 150 other state boards and commissions govern other state agencies over which the governor has little control. He or she may appoint members of these boards, but their terms fall vacant at staggered intervals and the governor must wait until terms expire before filling a vacancy. The boards usually appoint the agencies' executive directors, who actually manage the agencies. Some boards serve in nothing more than an advisory capacity. Therefore, the governor has only indirect appointive power over real administrators. The governor generally cannot issue direct orders to agencies. Even proposing a budget for agencies is largely the responsibility of the Legislative Budget Board rather than the governor.

The weak-governor system always raises the question of who is in control? Where is the supervision? What prevents overlap and duplication?

THE BUREAUCRACY AND PUBLIC POLICY

Administrators do more than simply administer policy. They actually make policy, because laws passed by the legislature often leave considerable room for administrative interpretation and flexibility. They make rules that are binding on the industries they regulate and the agencies they administer. In fact, the bureaucracy is deeply engaged in politics and strongly affects public policy.

Bureaucratic Power

To be effective, the bureaucracy must gain the political support necessary to accomplish its goals, increase appropriations, or even survive as an entity. The result of strong political support for an agency is increased size, jurisdiction, influence, and prestige. A less successful agency may suffer reduced appropriations, static or reduced employment, narrowed administrative jurisdiction, and possible extinction.

Where does a unit of the bureaucracy look for the political support so necessary to its well-being? It looks to clientele interest groups, the legislature, the chief executive, and the public. Political power also derives from internal factors in the bureaucracy, such as expertise, information, and discretion in the administration of the laws.

The Legislature   Bureaucratic power is enhanced through support by powerful legislators, often including the chair of the committee that oversees the agency. The agency is dependent on powerful legislative allies for laws that expand the powers of the agency, increase the scope of its duties, and appropriate the all-important funds for its operation. Therefore, administrators curry the favor of influential lawmakers. The importance of legislative support explains the intense lobbying that surrounds both the appointment of legislators to powerful legislative committees and the campaign activity that precedes election to positions of legislative leadership.

Clientele Groups   The most natural ally for an agency is its clientele (constituent) interest group—the group that benefits directly from agency programs. Ideally, the primary clientele group should be the public, but in practice powerful organized special interest groups have become the primary beneficiaries of most agency decisions. Agitation by these interest groups often leads to the initial establishment of an agency. The power and importance of an agency is often directly related to the influence of its clientele groups as well as to the intensity of their support. In Texas, some of the closer bedfellows are the Texas Good Roads and Transportation Association and Texas Department of Transportation; oil and gas industries and the Texas Railroad Commission; and the Texas Medical Association and State Department of Health.

Interest groups provide the mortar that cements the alliance between bureaucrats and legislators. Legislators rely on the support of interest groups for campaign financing. Interest groups often supplement legislators' incomes as well, especially in Texas, where legislative salaries are low. As time passes and the three-cornered coalition becomes more interdependent, each element looks to the others for support. The legislators bargain in the interests of the coalition; the agency bargains and fights for those same interests in the administration; and the special interest group assists with lobby support, campaign finances, and possible employment for legislators, ex-legislators, and former administrators.

The Chief Executive   The extent to which administrative agencies need the support of the chief executive depends on how successful the agency has been in finding other powerful political allies. Even when a governor has extensive administrative powers (as does the U.S. president), most agencies have considerable independence. In Texas, where the executive is decentralized and the governor has few direct administrative powers, administrative agencies are more likely to search for political allies among interest groups and powerful legislators. However, agencies still want the support of the governor, for a governor can influence the legislature when it considers appropriations bills and other matters important to the agency. The governor's item veto can also seriously affect an agency's funding.

The governor's cooperation is also important because of his or her appointive power. Agency employees develop shared attitudes, an esprit de corps, and a sense of communality with the employees of the agency's constituency interest groups. Because an agency's interests are usually similar to those of its constituency, both want the governor to appoint board members who will advance their mutual political goals.

Moreover, the governor's support gives the agency greater bargaining power with legislators and interest groups in achieving its goals. Although the Texas governor has few direct administrative powers, he or she can often help, delay, or thwart agency programs.

Public Support   Good public relations usually has a positive effect for any agency, both in its appropriations requests and in its battles with other agencies over jurisdiction. Broad public support—largely due to quality of public service or favorable propaganda—is enjoyed by some agencies such as the Texas Rangers. Unfortunately, no studies have been done in Texas concerning the nature and extent of state and local agency propaganda efforts.

Expertise   Administrators also possess a power inherent in any professional bureaucracy—knowledge and information. Policy-making officials in government can seldom be as well-versed in all the policy-making areas as are the bureaucratic personnel, who often have made a lifetime career of policy administration in a single area of governmental activity. The policymaker, whether appointed or elected, frequently has to rely on long-time government employees (who will be called on to administer the policy if it is enacted) for advice concerning contemplated public policy. Thus, those who are popularly perceived as only the administrators of the laws are often important forces in the genesis of those same laws.

The executive is also the branch of government that most often works directly with constituent interest groups, the general public, or both. Thus, bureaucrats serve as vehicles for gathering information in order to determine what laws are needed or wanted. Such information is invaluable to legislators as well as to other elected or appointed policymakers, but it is often available only at the discretion of top bureaucrats. In other words, bureaucrats may dispense information only if it will benefit their agency or clientele interest group. By the simple acts of giving and interpreting information, the bureaucracy influences the establishment of public policy.

Administration of the Laws   Interpreting and administering the laws provides another aspect of bureaucratic power. Administrative decisions not to enforce (or to enforce very leniently) consumer-protection, water-quality, or antitrust laws have the effect of deleting those laws from the statutes; the laws may remain in print indefinitely, but without enforcement they have no meaning. In this way, administrators have the power to establish policies that not only directly affect the lives of the general public, but essentially overrule the decisions of policy-making bodies.

Bureaucratic Accountability

The most recent challenge to responsible government has been the rise of a "bureaucratic state" in which appointed government agencies have a dramatic influence on citizens' personal lives. Given the size and political power of modern bureaucracy, the problem of administrative accountability is becoming even more acute. Various organizational arrangements and legal restrictions have been used in an attempt to make the administrative agencies accountable directly to the citizens, or at least to some official whom the citizens can hold responsible. To whom then should administrators be accountable?

Elective Accountability   The simplest approach has been to make the bureaucracy directly accountable to the people through the democratic process—the theory of elective accountability. This noble goal was to have been accomplished through the election of administrators by the voting public.

The problem involves the relative invisibility of elected executives. Very few voters are even aware of the names of the officeholders, much less the competence with which they are executing their duties. Thus, accountability to the general public through the election of administrators has evolved into a system of accountability to no one, and common incompetence or corruption goes unnoticed by an apathetic public.

Legislative Accountability   Some advocates of administrative reform argue that the bureaucracy should be accountable to the legislature; it is elected to protect constituent interests, and as legislators establish the policies, they are the ones who should determine if those policies are being administered according to legislative intent. This theory has been implemented by establishing legislative committees to oversee the administration, by conducting legislative investigations, and by establishing auditing and budgeting agencies under the control of the legislature.

There are weaknesses to this approach. Short sessions, as well as lack of adequate staffing and expertise, make continuing, independent supervision difficult. Campaign contributions from constituency interests may compromise the judgment of legislators. Also, because of the invisibility of the legislative decision-making process, the general public is not aware of policy decisions made by the committees. A most serious question about legislative supervision of the bureaucracy is "Who is watching the watchers?"

Accountability to the Chief Executive   Many reformers would like to see the Texas administration patterned after the cabinet system of the national government. Doing this would entail a reorganization and consolidation of the executive branch into larger subject-matter departments, with the governor being given power to appoint and remove top administrators and to propose a credible budget to the state legislature.

As no governor alone could control the dozens of agencies, their chiefs, and thousands of government employees, a bureaucratic organization such as the Executive Office of the President would have to oversee the administration and try to hold it accountable. This executive staff, although relatively invisible to the general public, would be accountable to the chief executive.

Theoretically, several benefits could result from accountability to the top executive. As his office is visible to the general public, the problem of "Who watches the watcher?" should be solved. If corruption or incompetence were apparent in the administration, there would be no question regarding ultimate responsibility. Administrative control would be simplified, resulting in coordinated planning and policy implementation.

This chain of accountability—from administrative agency to appointed executive to the staff to chief executive to the people—has one very weak link, however: the close ties between administrators, constituent interests, and key legislators. Interest groups would continue to influence administrative appointments and removals in "their" agencies, just as they now influence appointments to the boards and commissions. Even under a cabinet system, the governor would still have serious problems enforcing the accountability of those administrative agencies with powerful allies among interest groups and legislators.

Accountability to Interest Groups   To whom is an administrator really accountable? The answer is, in all probability, clientele interest groups. Politics work on the basic principles of mutual accommodation among allies and conflict among opponents. Agency officials are often obligated to administer the laws and make policy decisions in ways favorable to the goals and aspirations of their political allies among the private economic interests. Appointees, whether to boards or to administrative positions, usually are knowledgeable in the operational areas of the government agencies they serve. They are usually chosen from the industry concerned, and the policy decisions they make benefit most operatives in that industry. And where are government employees to seek employment once they leave government service? The natural job choice lies in the industry in which their expertise lies. With agency success, career success, and future employment often dependent on their actions while in the bureaucracy, many administrators feel that their primary accountability is to those economic powers most directly affected by them.

Administrative Accountability   How then can the Texas administration be made more accountable to the public? There is no single answer to this question. One solution is openness; a basic concept of democratic government is that policy made by government in the name of the public should be public knowledge. Granted, government needs to keep some national-security secrets, but too often the most closely guarded secrets have to do with administrative error, mismanagement, or even corruption. Bureaucratic employees could be rewarded (instead of being fired or demoted) for calling attention to bureaucratic excesses, blunders, or favoritism.

Also, *ombudsmen,* persons to handle specific citizen complaints and to assist people to navigate the bureaucracy, could be appointed. Two purposes could thus be accomplished: Administrative error or injustice could be rectified, and individual citizens might feel more trust in the efficiency of government.

Finally, agencies could be established to represent the consumer-citizen's interest alongside those of other government agencies and the economic giants of commerce, industry, and the professions. Consumers are a clientele interest group in search of an agency. As both legislators and bureaucrats represent private interests, it is imperative that the consumer also have representation, not only in the legislature, but in the bureaucracy as well.

CONCLUSION

The Texas governorship was conceived in the post-Reconstruction era, following an unfortunate and unhappy experience with a more centralized, alien, and unpopular state government. The formal powers of the office, and of Texas government as a whole, reflect this basic distrust of centralized government and of the executive branch in particular. The governor and the Texas legislature are weak when compared with those of other states. They are also weak when compared with other political forces in Texas.

This denial of power to the chief executive has created a power vacuum that has been filled willingly by interest groups and administrative agencies, which are basically non-elective institutions. Real power in Texas government rests with these institutions, and the legislature and governor frequently are able to ratify only those public-policy proposals advocated by dominant economic and other interest groups and their allies in the administrative agencies.

Government bureaucracies are usually officially organized in a hierarchy that provides for centralized control and accountability at the top. The lines of authority and communication are not followed in practice. The most notable characteristic of the Texas administration is that there is no single official responsible for the execution of policy. Numerous elected and appointed officials sit atop a multitude of little hierarchies and usually are responsible to no one in particular—except their clientele interest groups.

KEY TERMS

appointive powers

budgetary powers

bureaucratic
  accountability

chief of state

clemency powers

ex officio

formal powers

informal powers

message power

ombudsman

plural executive

pocket veto

removal powers

State of the State message

veto

veto override

Logging On

All statewide elected officials and most appointed boards have their own Websites. Governor Perry's site at **http://www.governor.state.tx.us/** gives examples of the latest gubernatorial decisions and allows students to receive the governor's latest press releases.

The lieutenant governor's site is at **http://www.senate.state.tx.us/**. The attorney general's is at **http://www.oag.state.tx.us/**. Comptroller of public accounts can be found at **http://www.cpa.state.tx.us/**.

Commissioner of the general land office is at **http://www.glo.state.tx.us/**. Commissioner of agriculture is at **http://www.agr.state.tx.us/**. Railroad Commission is at **http://www.rrc.state.tx.us/**. Texas Workforce Commission is at **http://www.twc.state.tx.us**.

The best and most citizen-friendly site for consumers of state services is at Texas Online (**http://www.state.tx.us/**).

7

Law, the Courts, and Due Process

INTRODUCTION

Law involves an attempt to impose one group's values onto others; it is a method of control. Some may be awed by the elegant language of the law, by the distinguished appearance of judges and their robes, or by the maneuverings of attorneys, but it is important to understand that *law is a tool to be used by those who write, interpret, and enforce it.* Law is indispensable to a civilized society, but it may also be cumbersome, arbitrary, or bureaucratic. To understand the practical operation of the Texas legal system, it is important to be familiar with several major categories of law.

CIVIL AND CRIMINAL LAW

There are substantial differences between criminal and civil law. Civil law deals largely with private rights and individual relationships, obligations, and responsibilities. Criminal law is concerned with public morality—concepts of right and

© Bob Daemmrich

An attorney addresses the jury in a civil trial.

wrong as defined by government. Thus, criminal cases are prosecuted by public officials (usually county or district attorneys) in the name of the public. Civil suits are brought by plaintiffs, who are usually private citizens or corporations, but agents of government occasionally initiate civil suits when seeking to enforce antitrust laws, abate public nuisances, and so forth.

Perhaps the most important distinction between civil and criminal law is in the way in which each prescribes *remedies,* the means used to enforce the law. Crime results in punishment; in civil law the remedy is relief or compensation. For example, criminal law might punish a thief, but the civil law remedy for the unlawful seizure of property might be the return of the property to its rightful owner. Juvenile proceedings, which are regarded as civil rather than criminal, are an interesting illustration of the difference between civil and criminal law. Assigning juveniles to the custody of reform schools is not intended as punishment, but as an effort to correct their delinquency. Assigning an adult to the penitentiary, however, is considered punishment.

Types of Civil Cases

Civil law in the states today is based in large part on centuries-old English *common law.* Common law is judge-made law; whether written or unwritten, it is based on *precedents.* If the essential elements of a current case are like those of a case already decided, the judge makes the same decision as was made in the earlier case. The principle of following these precedents is called *stare decisis,* and as a result, patterns have developed in court decisions that are the basis of common law. In contrast, *statutory law* is law that has been passed by legislative bodies and is written in code books. Legislatures have included many common-law principles in civil statutes and thereby reduced the need to rely directly on common law.

The family is protected by civil law in Texas. For example, even when a man and woman do not celebrate a formal ceremony of marriage in the presence of authorized officers of religious organizations or judges, the law may recognize the existence of a marriage. A man and a woman who live together with an agreement they are married and publicly present themselves as man and wife will have a *common-law marriage,* their children will be legitimate, and the marriage can be terminated through a legal divorce, or one year of separation.

Texas courts may require alimony between the filing and granting of a divorce, or when a spouse of at least ten years is incapable of self-support. Because Texas is a *community-property* state, its divorce law requires that a couple divide property acquired during marriage. Children have the right to be supported by their parents even if the parents are divorced. Either parent might be given legal custody of the children, but the other parent may be responsible for part of their support.

A person cannot lose title to a *homestead* in a civil suit except to satisfy tax liens, home-equity loans, or mortgage loans for initial purchase of the property. When private property is taken for public use, the owner is entitled to actual damages or its replacement value.

Even in death, property rights are protected: A person may direct transfer of his or her property through a will. Should a will exist at death, the function of the courts (usually the county courts) is to *probate* the will, which means to determine that it is the last and valid will of the deceased. If the deceased departed *intestate* (without leaving a will), civil law defines the right to inherit among various relatives; if there are no living relatives, the property passes to the state. The state may also recover certain Medicaid benefits from an estate, even if there is an heir.

Title to *real property* (land and buildings) is registered in the office of the county clerk, and the legitimate use of any property by its owner is enforceable in the courts. The right to inherit, bequeath, sell, lease, or transfer property is protected by law, but the rights of ownership do not include the privilege of misuse. The right to own a gun does not convey the right to use it as a weapon in murder; the privilege of opening an industrial plant does not include the right to pollute.

The regulation of private property for public purposes is one of the older functions of law. To that end, Texas law includes thousands of provisions and establishes hundreds of courts and administrative agencies to elaborate, interpret, and enforce them. State regulatory agencies include the Texas Railroad Commission, the State Insurance Commissioner, the Public Utilities Commission, and occupational licensing boards, among others. Their administrative regulations (*administrative law*) have the same binding effect as civil law and are usually enforceable in civil courts.

Corporations secure permission from the state to conduct their legitimate business; the secretary of state issues them a *charter,* which defines their structure, purposes, and activities. The secretary of state also issues permits to out-of-state corporations to operate in Texas. Civil law holds that upon the chartering of a corporation, a new legal person is created—one that can sue, be sued, or be fined for criminal activity.

The attorney general is responsible for bringing civil suits to seek *writs of injunction* (court orders compelling or prohibiting specific action) to end violations of the Texas antitrust and consumer-protection laws.

When two parties enter into a valid contract, the courts will enforce the terms of the contract. However, certain kinds of contracts are not enforceable in the courts—for example, a contract between minors, or a contract between labor and management that sets up a *closed shop* (management agrees to hire only labor-union members) or a *union shop* (management agrees to require all new employees to join the union as a condition for their continued employment).

Civil law also is designed to protect a person's reputation against false and malicious statements. *Slander* (spoken) or *libel* (published) may result in a suit to recover monetary compensation for any damages done.

A person whose negligence results in someone's bodily injury is liable for damages. The resulting personal injury suit would be based on an action in *tort* (a private or civil wrong or injury other than a breach of contract).

These are only selected illustrations. Texas civil law fills volumes of printed matter. Much of it is contained in *Vernon's Annotated Civil Statutes* and elsewhere. Obviously, it is impossible to discuss in detail the state's civil laws; even the most competent attorneys tend to specialize in specific fields of law.

Types of Crimes

As commonly used, the word *crime* refers to an act that violates whatever an authorized body (usually a state legislature) defines as the law. Many obey the law simply because it is law; others obey out of fear of punishment. Attitudes and values usually determine whether a person will respect or disobey a law. If a law reflects the values of most of society, as the law against murder does, then it is usually obeyed. However, if a large element of society does not accept the values protected by law, as was the case with national alcohol prohibition in the 1920s, or drug and gambling prohibition today, then violation becomes widespread.

Crime has become a national issue. But despite the popularity of "law and order" as a campaign slogan in national elections, only 5 percent of crimes are prosecuted under federal law. The activities of the criminal justice system are primarily state, not federal, functions. An act of Congress provides that federal offenses include only crimes (1) committed on the high seas, (2) committed on federal properties and reservations, (3) involving the crossing of state or international boundaries, (4) interfering with interstate commerce, or (5) committed against the national government or its employees while they are engaged in official duties. Otherwise, the vast majority of crimes are violations of state rather than federal law.

Felonies (Table 7.1) are serious crimes. Murder is the illegal, willful killing of another human being. Robbery is attempting to take something from a person by force or threat of force. It is inaccurate to say that "a house was robbed"—this literally means that a masked bandit stood at the front door with a pistol drawn on the doorbell and demanded that the building deliver up all its valuables. Instead, buildings are burglarized—unlawfully entered to commit a felony or theft.

T A B L E 7.1 Crime and Punishment Under Texas Penal Code[a]

Offense	Terms	Maximum Fine
Capital murder: Including murder of a police officer, firefighter, prison guard, or child under age six; murder for hire; murder committed during another felony such as rape, robbery, burglary, or arson, mass or terroristic murder	Execution or life sentence without parole.	
First-degree felony: Including aggravated sexual assault, theft over $200,000, robbery, murder, sale of more than 4 grams of "hard" drugs such as heroin	5 to 99 years	$10,000
Second-degree felony: Including theft over $100,000, burglary of a habitation	2 to 20 years	$10,000
Third-degree felony: Including theft over $20,000, drive-by shootings, involuntary manslaughter	2 to 10 years	$10,000
State jail felony: Including theft over $1,500, burglary of a building other than a habitation, sale of less than 1 gram of narcotics, auto theft, forgery	180 days to 2 years' probation[b]	$10,000
Class A misdemeanor: Including theft over $500, second-offense driving while intoxicated, resisting arrest, stalking	1 year maximum	$ 4,000
Class B misdemeanor: Including theft over $50, possession of small amounts of marijuana, reckless conduct (such as pointing a gun at someone), first-offense driving, flying or boating while intoxicated	180 days maximum	$ 2,000
Class C misdemeanor: Including theft under $50, smoking on a public elevator, disorderly conduct (such as indecent exposure)	None	$ 500

[a] Punishments may be reduced for murder committed in "sudden passion" or enhanced to the next level for crimes involving gang activity (three or more persons), the use of deadly weapons, previous convictions, or hate crimes (motivated by bias based on ethnicity, religion, or sexual orientation).

[b] Although probation must be granted, a judge may order a sixty-day jail sentence as a condition for probation. If the conviction is for narcotics, the jail term may be one year. Repeat offenders are no longer automatically given probation.

SOURCE: *Texas Politics Today,* 11 ed.

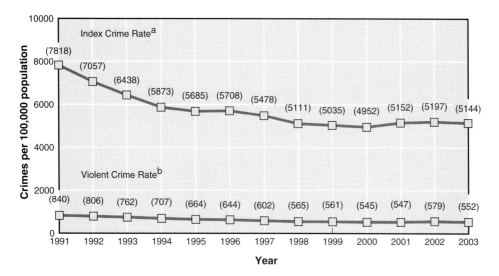

FIGURE 7.1 Texas Crime Rates Since 1991

SOURCE: Department of Public Safety, *Crime in Texas, Calendar Year* 2003 (Austin: Department of Public Safety, 2004), pp. 13–14.

Theft (larceny) is simply taking property from the rightful possession of another. Grand larceny—taking something valued over $1,500—is a felony. Regardless of value, livestock rustling (including shoplifting a package of bologna) is a felony. It is also a felony for a person to have sexual relations with a child under seventeen years of age unless the older partner is less than two years older than the younger.

In Texas it is a crime for a commercial fisherman to possess a flounder less than twelve inches in length. Betting on baseball games is outlawed. Even traffic violations are crimes, and the resulting fine is a form of punishment. Such minor crimes are called *misdemeanors,* punishable by a sentence in county jail and/or a fine (see Table 7.1).

Fortunately, Texas has experienced a long-term decline in the property crime rate (burglary, theft, and motor-vehicle theft) since its peak in 1988. The state's violent crime rate has also been declining since 1991, but it continues to produce violence-centered news coverage and general fear among Texans (see Figure 7.1).

THE COURTS

Trial and Appeal

Original Jurisdiction   Original jurisdiction is the power of a court to try a case. Trials involve following legal rules (applying the law) and viewing material evidence, examining documentary evidence, and hearing testimony that is evidence of *fact*. The judge oversees the legal procedure, but evaluating evidence is the jury's task (unless the right to a jury trial has been waived, in which case the judge also weighs the evidence). The verdict or judgment is determined and the remedy is set. Essentially, a trial answers questions of fact and law.

Appellate Jurisdiction   By contrast, appeal involves not a new trial, but a review of the law as it was applied in the trial itself. The mere fact that the prisoner may be actually innocent is not a basis for appeal. Many appeals are decided by review of the record (transcript) of the case and lawyers' written arguments (briefs); sometimes lawyers appear and present oral arguments. Appellate proceedings are based on law (legal process), not fact—no witnesses, material, or documentary evidence are presented. A reversal does not mean that the individual who was convicted is innocent; it means only that the legal process was improper. Thus, a person may be tried again in a court of original jurisdiction without question of double jeopardy, because the individual was never legally put in "jeopardy" the first time. If the appeals court reverses the lower court's decision, then no legal trial occurred.

Trial Courts' Jurisdiction

Municipal Courts   Most Texas trial courts (those with original jurisdiction) handle both civil and criminal matters. However, municipal courts try primarily minor criminal violations. As the cities' courts, they try violations of all city ordinances (punishable by fines up to $2,000). They also may hear violations of state laws for which the maximum penalty is a fine of $500 or less. The vast majority of their caseload involves traffic violations.

Justices of the Peace   Like municipal courts, justices of the peace (J.P.s) also devote most of their time to traffic tickets (usually those issued by agents other than city police). J.P.s share state criminal matters in which the maximum fine is $500. They may issue search warrants, conduct certain preliminary criminal hearings, and act as coroners. As coroners, they may determine cause of death in questionable cases, but this function is usually given to an appointed professional county medical examiner in urban counties. In civil matters, justices may decide cases involving disputes over less than $5,000. They also act as a court of small claims in which citizens argue minor disputes themselves without attorneys to represent them. Finally, J.P.s also conduct wedding ceremonies.

County commissioners establish from one to eight J.P. precincts in each county; each precinct then elects one or two justices for a four-year term. Commissioners also provide justices with limited salaries.

Most municipal courts and justices of the peace are not courts of record; thus, appeals based on the record are impossible. Completely new trials (trials *de novo*) may be granted by the county court, but many petitions for trials de novo result in the simple dismissal of charges because county courts are often overwhelmed by more serious legal business. Some cities have attempted to prevent such dismissals and lost revenues by having their municipal courts keep records, but this reform has not yet been made in any J.P. courts.

County Courts   In criminal matters, county courts have original jurisdiction over all misdemeanors more serious than those handled in municipal and J.P. courts. Crimes such as driving while intoxicated, possession of small quantities of marijuana, and the passing of bad checks exemplify crimes tried in county court. In general, county courts may handle trials for criminal cases in which punishment might include a fine in excess of $500 or a possible jail sentence. Although a majority of their cases involve such misdemeanors, county courts also handle such civil cases as financial disputes involving between $200 and $5,000, and probate (establishing the validity of wills).

County Courts-at-Law   The Texas constitution provides for only one county judge, who has jurisdiction throughout the county. However, in many of the more populous counties, the county judge has been unable to handle both the very large caseload and the many nonjudicial responsibilities assigned to the office. The legislature has thus established additional county courts-at-law to function as auxiliaries to the regular county courts. The jurisdiction of county courts-at-law varies according to the particular statute that established them. Most of them handle civil disputes under $100,000; some specialize in criminal or probate matters. While most counties have no county courts-at-law, the more populous counties may have several.

District Courts   The state's most important trial courts are the district courts, which have original jurisdiction over serious legal cases within their districts. Their criminal jurisdiction includes all felonies (punishment for which might include a stay in a state jail or penitentiary). However, a vast majority of district court cases are civil cases, such as divorces, juvenile cases, and disputes involving more than $200. In some of these civil cases, the district courts may share some jurisdiction with county courts and county courts-at-law.

District courts have jurisdiction within their districts, which are usually countywide; in some instances, several sparsely populated counties have been grouped together to form one district.

Appellate Jurisdiction

Courts of Appeal   Appeals from district and county-level courts initially go to one of fourteen courts of appeals. Each consists of three or more judges and has jurisdiction within its "supreme judicial district"—a geographical division established by the state legislature.

Texas Supreme Court   The nine-member Texas Supreme Court serves as the final court of appeals in civil cases from throughout the state. It also has original jurisdiction to issue certain writs, but it has no criminal jurisdiction.

Texas Court of Criminal Appeals   Final appeals in criminal matters are heard by the nine-member Texas Court of Criminal Appeals. It may review criminal cases that have been tried by district or county courts in the state. Figure 7.2 summarizes the jurisdiction of Texas's courts.

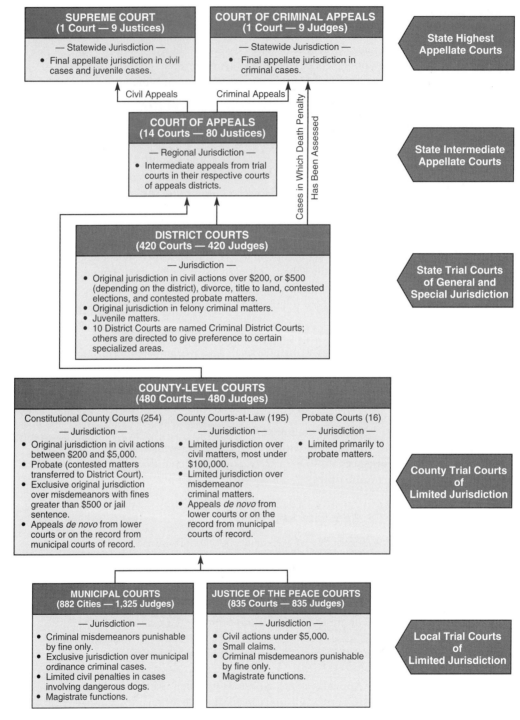

FIGURE 7.2 Court Structure of Texas

SOURCE: *Texas Judicial System Annual Report, 2003,* p. 32.

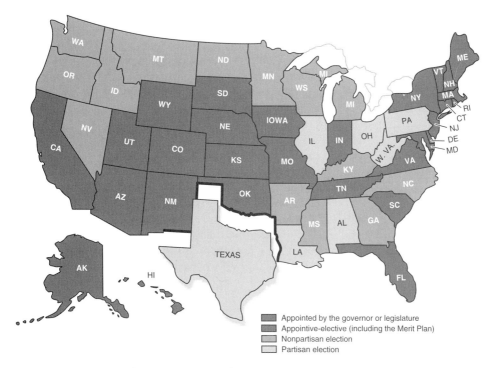

FIGURE 7.3 State-by-State Selection of Supreme Court Judges

SOURCE: Data from *The Book of the Sates, 2004* (Lexington, KY: Council of State Governments, 2004), pp. 250–253.

THE SELECTION OF JUDGES AND JURIES

Selection and Qualifications of Judges

Although Texas municipal court judges are usually appointed by city authorities, all other judges are elected by a partisan ballot. Having received their party's nomination in the primary, trial judges such as J.P.s, county judges, and district judges are elected in the general election for four-year terms. Judges on the multimember appellate courts (courts of appeals, Texas Supreme Court, and Court of Criminal Appeals) are elected for six-year overlapping terms.

Figure 7.3 shows that at least ten states, particularly Southern states, use partisan elections to select their appellate court judges. Although many other states also use this method to select trial judges, it has generated considerable controversy among lawyers and judges.

Partisan Election Although party labels may indicate judges' philosophical inclinations, Texas's partisan election of judges introduces political factors irrelevant to justice. Election, whether partisan or nonpartisan, subjects justice to the whims of campaigning in a popular democracy. In well-publicized cases, a judge seeking reelection may be tempted to make a decision because it is popular rather than just or legal.

Like other candidates for public office, elected judges must contend with factors such as image and personality, which may be unrelated to their qualifications and judicial talents. Their largest sources of campaign contributions were lawyers, Texans with special interests, particularly attorneys who may practice before the same judges they help to elect.

Generally plaintiffs' attorneys who represent consumers, minorities, patients, and workers contribute to Democratic candidates and lawyers defending business and insurance companies contribute to the Republicans. In 2002, for example, Republican candidates for the Texas Supreme Court outspent their Democratic rivals by more than three to one. Their largest single source of campaign contributions was lawyers, Texans for Lawsuit Reform (which supports limits on civil lawsuit awards), and other business groups. Earlier studies report similar findings that almost half of Supreme Court campaign contributions came from lawyers, about one-sixth from pro-business tort-reform groups, and about one-sixth from political action committees (PACs) and executives of fifty large corporations, most of whom represented sources that had cases pending before the Supreme Court.[1] Almost half of judges and 79 percent of attorneys believe campaign contributions have a significant impact on judicial decisions.[2]

Whether special-interest campaign contributions create a real conflict of interest or the mere perception of one, public perception of justice is at issue and public confidence in the system is at stake. Conflicts of interest occur as a direct result of election of judges, though the system represents a worthwhile attempt to hold judges responsible to the public.

Other methods for selecting judges can also be criticized. Appointment by the legislative or executive branch might allow judges to ignore their role as instruments of a democratic system. Charges of arrogance have been leveled against both federal judges and those in a few eastern states that use an appointive method. Once appointed, judges may become independent—too independent—of public opinion. Appointment also leads to "cronyism" and patronage—selection of officials based on friendships, favors, or political loyalty rather than objective qualifications.

The Merit Plan   Also known as the Missouri plan, or American Bar Association plan, this appointive-elective plan attempts to combine the advantages of both election (responsiveness to the public) and appointment (some degree of independence). It is also intended to place a major emphasis on qualifications. Under this plan, judges are nominated by eminent judges, lawyers, and legal scholars who form a committee to review legal qualifications. From this list of nominees the governor must select the judge for a short appointive term. Yet the public retains some influence because the end of a judge's appointive term is followed by an election in which voters decide whether to retain or reject the judge. Generally, the judge runs on the record of accomplishments while in office. In most states, challengers cannot file against the incumbent; extraneous campaign factors (including special-interest contributions) become less important.

Texas's Appointive-Elective System   Because many Texas judges dislike partisan election as provided by the Texas constitution, an informal mode of evading that method has developed. When they decide to retire, judges usually resign before the end of their term. Until the next election, the governor appoints those who fill state court vacancies and county commissioners fill vacancies occurring in county and J.P. courts. A majority of Texas judges were first appointed to their offices. Once selected, most judges win reelection without opposition, particularly because lawyers (who mostly finance judicial campaigns) are hesitant to oppose an incumbent judge. About 80 percent of judges are routinely reelected without opposition in Texas.

Thus, Texas has effectively adopted an appointive-elective system, but the state's failure to formally adopt the Merit Plan means that there is no formal judicial nominating committee made up of qualified professionals to screen prospective judges. The governor and county commissioners may use their power to fill vacancies for political or patronage purposes.

Qualifications   Appellate court judges must be relatively well qualified, having at least ten years' prior experience as a practicing attorney and/or judge in a court of record and being at least thirty-five years of age. A district judge must be a resident of the district for at least two years and a practicing lawyer or judge for at least four years. Fortunately, most serious legal matters are handled by these qualified judges.

Citizens with less "serious" legal business may justifiably feel they have been given a "kangaroo" trial. Judges of the county courts-at-law must be lawyers, but there is no such requirement for county judges, justices of the peace, or municipal judges. There is usually no record of proceedings in municipal or J.P. court. Once J.P.s were seriously biased because those people accused of crime paid a cost-of-court fee only if they were convicted. Although they continue to collect certain fees, counties now pay J.P.s a salary.

Selection of Trial (Petit) Juries

The right to a trial by jury is guaranteed in all Texas criminal cases as well as in most civil suits. Trial juries consist of six persons in lower-level trial courts or twelve persons in district courts. Jurors answer questions of fact and determine if the facts warrant a guilty verdict in criminal cases or a judgment in civil cases.

Jurors must be citizens, at least eighteen years of age, literate, and not convicted of or under indictment for a felony. The actual selection process begins as prospective jurors, the *venire,* are selected from lists of those with driver's licenses. Persons over sixty-five, students, and parents with custody of children under the age of ten may decline to serve. All others who are summoned may be required to serve, although the judge may excuse a person for excessive hardship.

Voir dire is initial questioning of prospective jurors by attorneys for each side to eliminate any juror for cause such as prejudice in the case. Attorneys for each party in the dispute are further given a number of *peremptory challenges,* or "strikes" (depending on the type of case), which allow the attorneys to dismiss prospective jurors on the basis of intuition rather than legal cause. Lawyers sometimes seek the advice of jury consulting firms, who study the inclinations and psychology of potential jurors.

Selection of Grand Juries

By contrast, *grand juries* are selected to review and investigate numerous criminal cases that might be presented during their term of three months or more. Rather than determining "guilt" or "innocence," the grand jury should serve as a check on prosecutors to prevent unwarranted prosecution. Individuals' freedom and reputations should be protected against trials based on flimsy evidence. A separate grand jury is not selected for each case, but serves several months and hears numerous cases presented by the prosecutor.

If the grand jury determines that the prosecutor has sufficient evidence to convict (a *prima facie* case), it will specify the charges in an *indictment*. The fact that a person has been indicted does not prove the accused guilty or innocent, and means only that the prosecutor has sufficient evidence to take the case to trial. Instead of hearing the defense, the secret grand jury sessions consider primarily the evidence in the hands of the prosecutor. Critics charge that the grand jury too often becomes a "rubber stamp" for the district attorney.

Because the right to indictment by grand jury is guaranteed only in felony cases, grand juries are associated with the district court, which has jurisdiction in such cases. A district judge will select a grand jury commission of three to five persons, who will nominate prospective grand jurors. From the list presented by the commission, the district judge selects twelve. Some district courts select grand juries randomly from the same lists as for trial juries.

CONCLUSION

Law is an instrument of those who write, interpret, and enforce it. It involves an attempt by the dominant elements of society to use government to impose their values on others.

Civil cases involve largely private rights and responsibilities. They are usually brought by private plaintiffs and involve a variety of issues such as torts, breach of contract, probate, and divorce. Civil cases constitute the majority of the workload of district courts and the fourteen courts of appeals, and they make up the Texas Supreme Court's entire docket. Meanwhile, minor crimes, or misdemeanors, are the primary work of municipal courts, justices of the peace, and county-level courts. Felonies are handled in district courts.

Except for municipal courts, trial judges are selected in partisan elections for four-year terms, and appeals court judges for six-year overlapping terms. However, judges are usually unopposed when they seek reelection, and when they retire before an election, the resulting vacancy is filled by an appointee of the governor or county commissioners, depending on the type of court.

Grand juries issue indictments to charge individuals in felony cases. Qualified members of grand juries may be selected randomly or by a grand jury commission. Petit (trial) juries determine verdicts and are selected from those having driver's licenses.

KEY TERMS

administrative law	grand juries	peremptory challenges
appellate jurisdiction	indictment	petit (trial) juries
civil law	misdemeanors	plaintiffs
common law	Missouri (Merit) Plan	precedents
criminal law	original jurisdiction	statutory law
felonies	partisan election	torts

Logging On

The courts of the state of Texas can be accessed at the Texas Judicial Server, located at **http://www.courts.state.tx.us/**.

The Texas Supreme Court is at **http://www.supreme.courts.state.tx.us/**. The Court of Criminal Appeals is at **http://www.cca.courts.state.tx.us/**.

Analysis of Texas Supreme Court decisions from the consumer viewpoint is at **http://www.texaswatch.org/**. Click on Court Watch. The Texas Department of Public Safety reports crime rates and factors contributing to crime at **http://www.txdps.state.tx.us/ucr/**.

ENDNOTES

1. Texans for Public Justice, http://www.tpj.org/press-releases/pr/html.

2. Texas Office of Court Administration, "The Courts and the Legal Profession in Texas—The Insider's: A Survey of Judges, Court Personnel, and Attorneys" (1998), http://www.courts.state.tx.us/publicinfo/publictrust/execsum.htm.

8

Local Governments: Their Structures, Politics, and Challenges

INTRODUCTION

Many so-called national issues can actually be traced to local problems. Until recently, national crime rates have been skyrocketing, but crime is largely a neighborhood affair, primarily the responsibility of the local sheriff's department or the city police. On the national level, there have been startling declines in student achievement, but education is primarily the responsibility of local school districts. Urban traffic jams and the smog they produce are found in the streets and roadways built by our cities. From the physical decay represented by slums to social or moral decay, many of our problems are most manageable at their places of origin. What are considered national challenges are really unsolved local problems that are out of control and have therefore become a national concern.

Yet many local services are performed so well that people often take them for granted. Local governments still light and maintain our streets; we only remember the potholes. Local governments often collect our garbage, but we are most likely to recall the flies last Tuesday. Cities may light our homes and drain our lavatories, but the blackouts come to mind. Our locally serviced or regulated water almost never goes dry. In fact, local governments probably affect our daily lives more directly than state or national government, but many of their functions are performed so well we are scarcely aware of them. Many expectations are met so well that they are ignored, but failures become the focus of national attention.

A single vote or citizen's complaint can have more impact at the local level than at any other, but citizen awareness remains a major problem for local government. The local news media generally focus little attention on local governments, particularly counties, small cities, and special districts. The large number of local governments may be a further source of citizen confusion; students may be surprised to learn that there are so many local governments in the United States that the national government conducts a census of governments, in which it counts government much as it counts people. The U.S. Census Bureau[1] reports that Texas has the following 4,784 local governments

Counties	254
Cities	1,196
School districts	1,089
Other special districts	2,245, including

    metropolitan transit authorities

    water districts

    hospital districts

    housing authorities

    river authorities

    municipal water districts

    hospital districts

    housing authorities

    river authorities

    municipal utility districts

    soil conservation and reclamation districts

    flood-control districts

    navigation districts

    rural fire prevention districts

    airport authorities

    jail districts

    emergency-services districts.

With such an overwhelming number of local governments, many are small, with limited jurisdiction, performing only a few services and functions. Citizens may find it nearly impossible to even know all the districts that exist, let alone what they do or how well they do it. The structures of some local governments further add to the puzzle; many have numerous appointed or elected officials without distinct, unified lines of executive responsibility. This chapter will present the structure, power, politics, and problems of the many local governments in Texas.

COUNTIES

Although counties have been called the "dark continent" of American politics, they were once the most important type of local government. Even today, residents of rural areas consider counties "their" government.

Origin

Like so many elements of American government, counties can be traced to the influence of the British, who established county government first in Virginia, a full century and a half before the United States itself was established. From there migrants carried the concept of county government both south and west, where it became the dominant form of rural local government. "Towns" and "townships" were established side by side with counties in New England, in the Middle Atlantic states, and in the Midwest, but in some ways both towns and townships performed the same functions as county governments.

Although Louisiana uses the term "parishes" and Alaska uses "boroughs," county government has spread to forty-eight states—only the two smallest states (both in New England), Rhode Island and Connecticut, manage without counties. New England counties have been less important, and the two smallest states seem to need no such subdivisions to function. In fact, the entire state of Rhode Island (1,049 square miles) is about the size of the typical Texas county. Brewster County, Texas, is almost six times as large (6,208 square miles).

With 254 counties, Texas claims the distinction of having not only more counties than any other state (more than four times as many as the average state), but also some of the most sparsely populated in the nation (including the nation's least populated, Loving County, whose population of 67 is outnumbered by cows by more than 24 to 1). Modern Texans may not understand the need for so many counties without looking at their original purposes.

Purpose

Since their beginning, counties were designed to offer government services at a locally accessible level and to impose government control on citizens where they lived. Not only were Texans once migrants, mostly from the older Southern states, familiar with county government, but Texas is extremely large in area. There was an obvious need to decentralize its functions under local control. Population was small and long-distance communication was almost nonexistent. Most Texas counties were laid out so that the typical citizen lived no more than one day's horse-and-buggy ride to and from the county seat. The current structure of Texas county government was mostly established by the Texas Constitution of 1876. With less than 20,000 people, San Antonio was the largest city in Texas, essentially a rural state. In less than a single century, between the 1830s and 1930s, agricultural Texas established all of its counties.

The attributes that helped counties so effectively fulfill their roles in an earlier era, are today criticized for being out of step with the times.

1. Counties are too small to be efficient.
2. Many county offices are no longer needed and are of little interest to the metropolitan Texan.
3. Counties are rigidly structured and not able to adapt to Texas's modern, urban environment.

Functions

Texas counties are created largely to perform state functions such as

1. Collecting certain state taxes and fees—for example, the 6.25 percent sales tax on automobiles.
2. Administering and financing state elections, both general and special.
3. Maintaining records for the state—deeds, marriage licenses, contracts, wills, mortgages, election returns, etc.
4. Enforcing state law—the sheriff's office has been primarily responsible for enforcing *Texas law* with some assistance from locally elected constables (also officers of the county). City police have assumed much of this function in urban areas, but county officers remain the protectors of law and order in rural areas.
5. Convicting violators of state law and handling minor civil cases by county-level judges and justices of the peace. Counties also provide office space for state district judges and supplement their salaries.
6. Prosecuting violators of state law by the county or district attorney, both largely county officers.
7. Registering automobiles.

Counties continue to perform limited functions with respect to transportation and welfare. Road- and bridge-building was once a major county function and, despite state farm-to-market roads, the counties largely remain responsible for transportation in rural areas. Counties also provide certain welfare services, which vary from county to county. In addition, there are certain functions that are optional for the county, for example,

1. Establishing county libraries.
2. Operating public cemeteries.
3. Financing and managing a county hospital and other health services.

4. Adopting a county unit road system.

5. Establishing a county civil service system.

6. Creating a county community college district.

7. Providing some parks, airports, and a few welfare programs.

8. Contracting with other local governments to provide various public services such as fire protection and emergency medical services.

Ironically, the state is highly dependent on counties for many services, but has little means to control them.

1. Although the legislature created the counties, the constitution prohibits it from abolishing them, moving their county seat, or changing their boundaries except under strictly limited circumstances.

2. More important, most major and (some minor) county functions and offices are established by the constitution, so change requires the difficult process of amending the state constitution. Some changes can be made by statutes passed by the state legislature. There is no provision for county home rule and ordinary voters are generally denied the right to change the function and structure of counties.

3. While the county is required to perform many functions for the state, the local county commissioner's court determines the county's tax rate and how much will be spent for each activity.

In short, the state constitution and statutes determine many county functions (what will be done), but financing and supervising each function is a local matter.

Organization

Which county officers perform these varied functions? The answer, by no means simple, is scattered among numerous constitutional provisions and statutes. Furthermore, county functions are extremely decentralized, because so many elected and appointed county officers share in the decision-making process. There is no single "chief executive" for the county.

It is useful to classify official functions as being legislative (general policy-making), executive (carrying out policies made by state and county authorities), or judicial (largely interpreting laws for the state and applying them to specific cases). Explaining county government in terms of these three functions should not leave the impression that they are distinct. Like most other types of local government, counties are not characterized by a clear-cut separation of powers. There is considerable sharing of powers, and one official may take on more than one function. In fact, the county judge is a "jack-of-all-trades," performing legislative, executive, and judicial functions.

Legislative Officials   The *county commissioners' court* is by no means a court; instead, it is the legislative, policy making body for the county. Commissioners' court consists of four *county commissioners* and the *county judge,* who presides and votes at meetings of the commissioners' court. Commissioners are elected for four-year overlapping terms from precincts established by the county commissioners' court. The county judge is elected countywide for a four-year term.

Although the county commissioners' court has limited power to pass ordinances, it performs legislative functions when it establishes certain general policies for the county, such as the following:

1. Setting the tax rate. The largest single source of county revenue is the *ad valorem* (according to value) tax on property. Although this tax is usually applied to real property (land and buildings), it may also apply to such personal property as automobiles or boats. Within the constitutional maximum of 80 cents tax per $100 of property value, the commissioners' court sets the tax rate. At its discretion, it may also tax any occupation that is taxed by state government.

2. Adopting the budget. In addition to funding the many services and functions required by the state, the commissioners *may* fund certain optional programs.

3. Providing for the construction or leasing of such buildings and facilities as are required for county operations.

4. Establishing county electoral districts. Commissioners' court draws the boundaries for voting precincts, justice of the peace and constables' precincts, and the commissioners' own electoral precincts of approximately equal population.

Executive Officials   The Texas Constitution was written in reaction to abuses of power, particularly executive power, during Reconstruction following the Civil War. As a result, framers of the constitution divided executive power within counties as much as at the state level. Rather than providing for a chief executive, administrative responsibilities are decentralized among numerous county officers—some of them are appointed, but many are elected for four-year terms.

Commissioners' Court   In addition to its legislative functions mentioned earlier, county commissioners' court has several executive duties, including

1. Appointing certain county boards and officers, such as the county health officer, the county road engineer (if the office has been established), the county home demonstration agent, etc.

2. Filling vacancies in elective offices that might occur before a scheduled election.

3. Letting contracts for county projects such as building jails, public buildings, etc.

4. Designating polling places, election judges and clerks, and canvassing election returns.

In addition to these collective duties, each commissioner is usually responsible for building and maintaining county bridges, roads, and parks within his or her individual precincts. Some of the larger urban counties have eliminated duplication and inefficiency by establishing a unit-road system under a county engineer who supervises a countywide program. However, in rural counties, commissioners often find that road-building can be a source of political power—hiring and dismissing the road crew, purchasing materials, and rewarding supporters with well-maintained roads.

Considering all of its formal powers, commissioners' court is probably the most powerful county institution. The power to adopt a budget is particularly important, because most other county officers depend on the commissioners as their exclusive source of funds. Therefore, commissioners often develop informal controls over many county offices, even though they lack any formal power to select, remove, or direct elective county officers.

County Judge   In his or her legislative role as presiding officer over county commissioners' court, the county judge may develop considerable prestige as the only policymaker elected countywide. He or she may be in a unique position to negotiate compromises among the commissioners or other county officers. However, the county judge also has executive responsibilities such as

1. Filling vacancies on commissioners' court.

2. Preparing a proposed budget for ultimate consideration and approval by commissioners' court. In more populous counties, this function has been assumed by the county auditor.

3. Handling certain election tasks such as posting election notices, receiving election returns from the election judges, and preparing them for canvassing by county commissioners' court.

4. Serving on or appointing members to serve on certain county boards such as the juvenile board or county hospital board.

Law-Enforcement Officers   Alongside the county judge and commissioners, the county *sheriff* is elected for a four-year term and is usually considered among the more powerful of county officers. In urban counties he or she may have a relatively large budget and staff of deputies to assist in enforcing state law throughout the county, but the sheriff usually refrains from patrolling city streets, in order to avoid conflicts with the city police departments. The sheriff's department also operates the county jail, and delivers and executes court process (such as serving court orders).

Constables, elected for four-year terms from the same precincts as justices of the peace, serve as general law-enforcement officers. They also keep order in justice of the peace courts, deliver court process, and take on private security duties. Some counties have abolished this office and merged its functions into the sheriff's department.

Financial Officers   Among several financial officers for the county, the *county tax assessor-collector* is elected for a four-year term and is probably the most important. The tax assessor-collector

1. Collects various county taxes and fees, including the important county *ad valorem* (property) tax.

Courtesy of the Office of the County Judge, County of El Paso.

County Judge Dolores Briones.

2. Collects certain state taxes and fees, particularly motor-vehicle registration fees (license-plate fees), and the motor-vehicle sales tax.

3. Contracts with other local governments to collect property taxes on their behalf.

4. In some counties, also registers voters.

The assessor-collector once had considerable discretion in deciding what to tax and its value. The assessor's friends and political allies often benefited from lower evaluations. Today, however, all local governments must use appraisals conducted by the central appraisal district in each county.

Elected for a four-year term, the county *treasurer* performs functions as a financial officer by receiving, depositing, and disbursing county funds. In all but the smallest counties, a county *auditor* is appointed by the district judges for a two-year term. The auditor reviews all county financial records and countersigns warrants issued by the treasurer's office. Some counties have abolished the treasurer's office and placed all of its functions in the auditor's office. In larger counties, the auditor also assumes the county judge's role as chief budget officer.

Clerical Officers The *county clerk,* elected for a four-year term, serves as the county's chief record keeper and election officer. The county clerk's duties include

1. Serving as clerk for the county commissioners' court.

2. Maintaining records for justices of the peace and county courts.

3. Recording deeds, mortgages, wills, and contracts.

4. Issuing marriage licenses and maintaining certain records of births and deaths.

5. Serving on the county election board, certifying candidates running for county office, and carrying out other "housekeeping" functions in connection with elections, except where these functions have been assigned to a county election administrator.

Most counties elect the *district clerk* for a four-year term to maintain records for district courts and manage their caseloads (dockets). Some counties have both district and county clerks who specialize in various record-keeping functions for the courts.

Legal Officers Counties may have either a *county attorney* or a *district attorney,* or both. Where there is only one, the official prosecutes all criminal cases, gives advisory opinions to county officials, and represents the county in civil proceedings. If a county has both a district and a county attorney, the district attorney specializes in prosecuting cases in district court, while the county attorney handles lesser cases.

Miscellaneous Executive Officers There are still more executive officers for the county. Elected for a four-year term are a county *surveyor,* a county *weigher,* and even a county *inspector of hides and animals.* Most counties may authorize such appointive officers as the county health officer, county medical examiner, county agricultural agent, home demonstration agent, and county election administrator.

Judicial Officials County judicial officers include one to sixteen *justices of the peace,* one *county judge,* and perhaps a number of *county court-at-law judges.* Each is elected for a four-year term and is paid from county funds. Although *district judges* are paid primarily by the state, they must also be considered county officials, because they perform such county functions as appointing the auditor, and they are given office space and salary supplements by the county commissioners. Like many county officers, these judges perform functions for the state and handle criminal violations and civil cases arising under state law. Figure 8.1 illustrates the structure of county government.

Reform

There has been extensive criticism of county government in Texas. Wholesale reform, however, seems unlikely because powerful county officials frequently resist changes. They have usually opposed consolidation of city and county functions and county home rule (allowing voters to reorganize county government).

Statutory and constitutional provisions that establish the functions and structure of county government are quite rigid. Although the county may establish certain optional offices and programs, the structure of county government is fairly standardized: Harris County, with a population of 3,400,578, operates under the same basic structure as Loving County, population 67. It takes little imagination to see that Loving and Harris counties have developed different problems and needs. However, it is not likely that counties, with their rural origins, can be

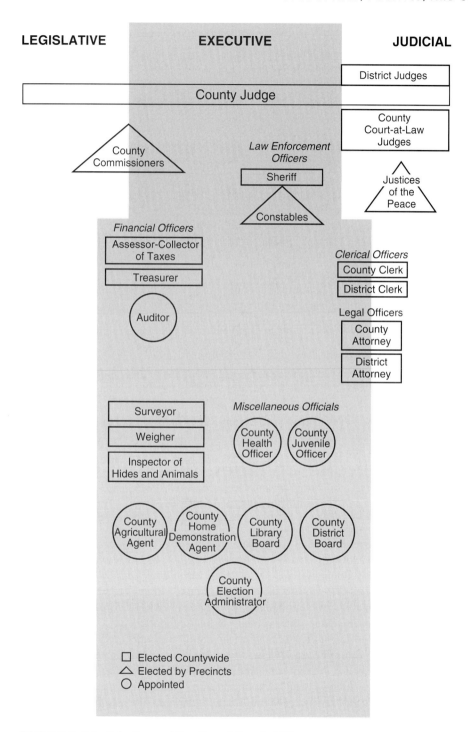

FIGURE 8.1 Selection and Function of County Officers

easily adapted to become essential solutions to metropolitan problems, as some reformers demand.

Most criticism has focused particularly on executive offices in county government. There is no chief executive to exercise leadership or oversee county administrative officials. Public perception of corruption and inefficiency is directly linked to the absence of such overhead supervision.

It is naive to assume that major county officers will be responsible simply because they are elected by voters. The voter is bewildered and confused by the *long ballot* and is frequently bored by the number of candidates seeking minor, routine decision-making positions. As a result, turnout is low and voters are often uninformed. Reformers suggest shortening the ballot by allowing minor officers to be appointed by a highly visible county executive whom voters can hold responsible for the actions of his or her subordinates.

Additional criticism has resulted from the decentralized county structure. Generally, each county officer is responsible for hiring his or her office employees. The *spoils system* (hiring political supporters) continues to operate, and workers are often selected for their political talents rather than their skills and efficiency at the job. Larger counties *may* establish a county civil service (merit) system. Even in the few counties using such a system, powerful county officers have been able to bypass its intent.

Most county officers not only hire their own employees, but they usually make purchases for their departments. A few counties centralize purchasing in the auditor's office. Reformers suggest that this be made a requirement in all counties so they can buy in bulk and effectively bargain with contractors.

CITIES

Development of the Cities

In America's growing metropolitan areas, age-old problems take on new dimensions. The danger of fire in densely populated areas was virtually ignored until fires around the early 1900s in relatively new cities such as Chicago and San Francisco. Disease in sparsely populated areas is generally an individual problem; in urban areas it may become a communicable hazard. Terrorism in the last few years has produced incalculable costs and dangers for cities. Poverty and racism always pose serious problems for their victims, but in densely populated areas individual suffering feeds the misery of others until the compound effect is the rejection of the culture that nurtured the problem, a rejection reflected in protest, crime, and even wholesale riots. A dilapidated farmhouse is a problem to the tenant; a similar structure in a large city is a neighborhood menace. Urbanization means that people must be transported in unprecedented numbers; consequently, cities turn to modern modes of transportation, whether it be the expressway or the subway. Population growth and urbanization lead to political problems. Simply living together in large numbers is difficult, and cities must handle these issues.

Texas cities are generally newer than those in the rest of the nation, yet Texas has become one of the most urban states in the union—approximately 80 percent of Texans now live in cities. It is clear that Houston, Dallas, and San Antonio are major American cities. In fact, many of their suburbs, such as Arlington, Garland, Irving, and Pasedena, have larger populations than important older Texas cities such as Galveston or San Angelo. Because urban development has been so recent, many Texans still identify with their rural origins and have moved to the outskirts of major cities (exurbia) and drive extremely long distances to shop and work. Extreme traffic congestion results in metropolitan areas.

For several reasons, Texas cities have been able to avoid some of the problems that have plagued older cities in other regions of the nation. Although Texas cities include some deteriorating neighborhoods, their relative youth means that urban decay is less evident in Texas central city areas. Expanding commerce and industry and increasing population have allowed Texas's urban communities to finance essential services. Also, municipalities have been able to expand their boundaries because of the generous annexation powers granted them by the state legislature.

On the other hand, certain problems are especially severe in Texas cities. Crime rates are higher than in most of the rest of the nation. Many cities are experiencing rapid population increases and must finance new services and infrastructure in growing areas.

Legal Status

Cities, like other local governments, are legally considered creations of the state. As a result, courts usually resolve any conflict between state and local policy in favor of the state.

Incorporation   Actually, general laws and the home-rule provisions in the state constitution provide cities with a degree of flexibility not available to counties. And, although cities are established under the general authority of the state, the actual process of incorporation (forming a city, which is a *municipal corporation*) is accomplished by citizen initiative. A community of more than 200 persons may submit a petition to the county judge; the judge will call an incorporation election if the petition is in order and signed by a number of registered voters determined by the type of city to be formed.

Annexation   Once incorporated, a city has broad powers within its city limits; it may even apply certain building and zoning ordinances beyond its city limits, the *extraterritorial jurisdiction* (ETJ). See Table 8.1 for an idea of the area covered. The size of the ETJ depends on the city's population.

Although cities may not impose taxes in their ETJ, home-rule cities may notify and annex any unincorporated community or part of it *without* permission of residents or property owners, as long as the area annexed annually does not exceed 10 percent of the city's existing territory. Even if a city fails to use its 10 percent quota, it may later annex the unused portion of territory (but not more than 30 percent in any three-year period).

TABLE 8.1   Area of Cities' Extraterritorial
                     Jurisdiction

Population of City	ETJ Beyond Its City Limits
Less than 5,000	$^1/_2$ Mile
5,000–25,000	1 Mile
25,000–50,000	2 Miles
50,000–100,000	$3^1/_2$ Miles
Over 100,000	5 Miles

No community may incorporate or annex within the ETJ of another city. Hence, some smaller communities have incorporated as cities in order to prevent larger metropolitan areas from bringing them into the larger area's ETJ or annexing them.

It is clear that suburbs benefit from being a part of the metropolitan community and take advantage of central city services such as streets, libraries, sports stadiums, and business subsidies. Frequently, affluent Anglos have fled to the suburbs, leaving the poor and ethnic minorities to finance the expensive metropolitan services. Meanwhile, suburbanites may pay much lower tax rates to support their local communities' voluntary fire departments, small police forces, and the like.

In certain metropolitan areas of the Northeast, as many as 70 percent of the residents live outside the central city. In effect, these suburbs have suffocated the central city, which cannot expand beyond the suburbs that encircle it. The inevitable results are financial problems and urban decay. However, generous annexation laws have allowed most Texas cities to escape much of this fate. Among major Texas cities, Dallas best fits the national pattern, although it is far less troubled than such cities as Boston, Cleveland, Washington, D.C., New York, or Detroit. By contrast, much of Houston's growth has been recent—it has been able to expand into outlying residential developments.

Structure

During early Texas history, cities were incorporated by special acts of the legislature that specified municipal structure and function. Legislative charters were often granted as special favors, and bribery was not unknown.

In 1858, the legislature took the first step in eliminating such special treatment. Cities that met uniform requirements were permitted to accept a standardized structure established by *general law.* However, special legislative charters for larger cities continued to consume the legislature's time. On the other hand, standard regulations did not permit cities sufficient flexibility to adapt to local needs and conditions.

Home-Rule Cities   In 1912, the Texas Constitution was amended to include *home rule,* permitting cities with a population of over 5,000 to write, approve, and amend any charter provisions that did not violate the constitution or other state laws. Special legislative charters were thereby eliminated, because the legislature by this time required smaller cities to incorporate under general law.

Some communities fear the increases in power and tax authority granted to home-rule cities and continue to operate under general laws even when their population exceeds 5,000 and would allow home rule. For these reasons, several cities with populations over 5,000 still operate under general laws. Texas has about 300 home-rule cities.

General-Law Cities   All municipalities of less than 5,000 and those larger cities that have not adopted home-rule charters continue to operate under general laws. They may choose from among several structures.

If a general-law city selects the *aldermanic form,* it may elect as many as five aldermen for one- or two-year overlapping terms. Whether the aldermen are elected *at-large* (city-wide) or from *wards* (from neighborhood districts or precincts), the mayor is elected at-large and presides over and votes at meetings of the board of aldermen. As the policy-making (or legislative) body for the city, the board adopts the budget, adopts ordinances, and may authorize the appointment or election of various administrative (or executive) officers such as a city marshal, city clerk or secretary, and zoning commission. As one of the city's administrative officers, the mayor signs contracts and ordinances and performs such other administrative duties as the board of aldermen may direct. The mayor often serves as the municipal judge.

By contrast, the *commission form* requires the election of two commissioners and a mayor. Together, they form the general governing body for the city, passing ordinances and designating various officers who administer city programs. As with the aldermanic form, there are several options as to which offices will be established to administer specific programs.

When a majority of voters approve, the governing body may select a manager to handle the general administrative responsibilities for the city.

Forms of City Government   Under each form, the general laws now offer cities numerous options as to both structure and form. Similar options exist in other states for their cities, so there are literally thousands of different city charters across the nation. To simplify the task of studying city government, political scientists have classified cities into several categories based on the nature of legislative-executive relations and the role and power of the executive. There is a considerable amount of overlap among these characteristics.

Mayor-Council Form   Although this form of government is not so popular among Texas cities, a majority of our nation's larger cities often use it. Houston is one major Texas city that uses this type.

Under the mayor-council form, the *council* may consist of between three and a dozen or so members; they may be elected at-large, by wards, or by a combination of both. Regardless of its size or manner of election, the council serves as the *legislative branch* of the city's government. It makes general policy by

1. Adopting ordinances; city law in Texas is of the criminal variety and punishment is by fines up to $2,000.
2. Setting the tax rate.

3. Establishing city programs and services.

4. Approving the municipal budget.

5. Making rules and regulations for carrying out programs and providing services.

6. Creating such optional offices as may be allowed by the city charter.

The *mayor* is at least the symbolic head of the *executive* branch; however, the mayor's capacity to actually control or manage city agencies varies widely from city to city. Scholars usually subdivide the mayor–council category according to the mayor's power.

STRONG-MAYOR TYPE   This form of city government, which most closely parallels that of the national government, is the only form in which there is a clearly *distinguishable separation of powers,* because its charter usually forbids the council from intervening in the daily affairs of the executive branch. The mayor, who is usually elected independently from the council in a citywide election, has the basic powers of a *true chief executive.*

1. The authority to appoint, remove, and direct heads of most city departments. These powers are considered essential for effective management, planning, and control of any organization, whether business, government, or education.

2. The power to propose a budget to the city council. Although the city council must finally adopt the budget, each department must submit budget requests through the mayor's office—city administrators do not present budget requests directly to the city council without permission of their "boss." The mayor's budgetary power can be used to control subordinate bureaucrats whose prestige and power depend on how much money their agencies spend.

3. The prerogative of representing city agencies in nonbudgetary matters pending before the council. The mayor's influence over the council is usually increased by the fact that the mayor has the power to preside over council meetings, veto ordinances, and appeal to public opinion.

Because of the mayor's powers to control executive departments, this form is characterized by *unified lines of executive responsibility.*

WEAK-MAYOR TYPE   This form involves a more restricted legislative and executive role for the mayor. Although the weak mayor is usually selected at-large (rather than by the council) and may preside at council meetings, the mayor usually lacks *formal* powers to affect council decisions, such as the veto or effective budgetary controls. A few mayors have developed considerable personal political prestige in spite of charter provisions; many are little more than ceremonial leaders.

The weak mayor is not a genuine chief executive, because several independent city officials share power in the executive branch. The weak mayor may appoint, remove, and direct a few department heads, but many important city officials are selected by means independent of the mayor's control, such as

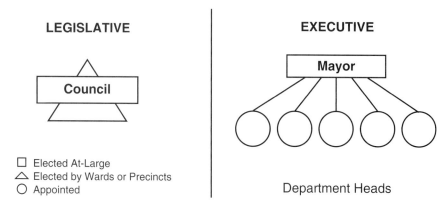

LEGISLATIVE

□ Elected At-Large
△ Elected by Wards or Precincts
○ Appointed

FIGURE 8.2a Strong-Mayor Council Type

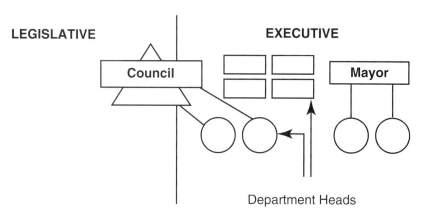

FIGURE 8.2b Weak-Mayor Council Type

1. Election directly by voters
2. Appointment by city council
3. Service *ex officio*

The weak-mayor form lacks unified lines of administrative responsibility. Although not frequently used by Texas cities, in many ways this form resembles that of Texas state government with its *plural executive system*. Figure 8.2 illustrates the strong- and weak-mayor forms.

Commission Form A small number of commissioners (about five) are elected citywide; they handle both legislative and executive functions for the city. Collectively, the commission is the general policy-making body, passing ordinances, adopting the budget, setting the tax rate, and the like. Individually, each commissioner handles one or more executive functions and heads particular administrative departments.

The commission form is now mostly of historical interest. It was developed in Galveston in response to the great hurricane that struck the city around the turn of the twentieth century. Reformers helped spread this simple structure throughout the United States. Today, however, it has become almost extinct; most cities that used this form (including Galveston itself) have transformed it to the council-manager form.

Council-Manager Form   Nationally, the council-manager form is used primarily in smaller cities. In Texas, it is clearly the most popular form even among many larger cities. San Antonio and Dallas are two of the largest cities in the nation to use this form. With this type of city government, the council is the legislative body, but it also has the power to select and dismiss the *city manager,* who serves as the city's chief administrator or executive. Ultimate legislative and executive responsibilities are combined in a single institution. However, individual council members may not intervene in the *daily* course of city administration as in the commission form. Lines of executive responsibility converge in the manager's office, but the council evaluates the manager's overall performance.

As chief administrator, the manager

1. Appoints, directs, removes, and supervises major department heads.
2. Recommends the annual budget (including the tax rate) to the council for its approval.
3. Conducts investigations and evaluative studies of city operations and reports to the council.
4. Suggests ordinances and policy changes deemed useful.
5. Supervises routine financial dealings such as purchases and disbursements.

The council-manager system has a reputation for efficiency for the following reasons:

1. The manager is usually a professional, trained in public administration.
2. Because the manager usually has no power base in the community, he or she can be easily dismissed or otherwise held responsible to the council.
3. Because he or she is not a politician, the manager can make decisions with an eye toward efficiency, rather than satisfying powerful interests or attracting votes.
4. When reformers succeed in installing the council-manager form, they often institute a *merit system* for hiring employees based on their qualifications to replace the *spoils system* in which employees were hired because of their political opinions or campaign support.

Although the council-manager form has a reputation for efficiency, it frequently suffers from a *lack of effective political leadership.* The manager, though the chief executive, cannot use his or her powers to gain effective political influence with community leaders or the general public. The *mayor,* selected by the council or in an at-large election, serves as the ceremonial leader of the city—clipping ribbons, welcoming visiting dignitaries, representing the city at miscellaneous

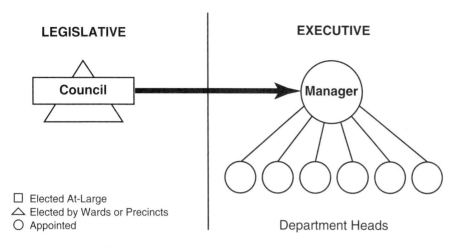

LEGISLATIVE   **EXECUTIVE**

☐ Elected At-Large
△ Elected by Wards or Precincts
○ Appointed

Department Heads

F I G U R E   8.3   The Council-Manager Form

conferences, and so on. The mayor's formal, official powers are usually confined to serving on the council and presiding at its meetings, but the publicity that surrounds the mayor's office and its ceremonial duties still allow a strong personality to develop some effective political leadership. (Figure 8.3 illustrates the council-manager structure.)

Mayor-Manager Form   Also known as the mayor–administrator form, this system combines certain essential elements of the council-manager and strong-mayor forms in an attempt to promote both strong leadership and efficient administration.

   A separation of powers results from placing the manager under the control of the mayor rather than the council. Of course, the council retains its legislative prerogatives, but administration is placed in the hands of the mayor and manager. The mayor may become an effective leader because he or she has most of the powers of the strong mayor and may also hire and fire the manager, the mayor's chief administrative assistant. The mayor leaves most routine administrative decisions to the professional manager, but has ultimate control over the administrator and, hence, the executive branch. (Figure 8.4 illustrates the mayor-manager system.)

Evaluating City Government and Politics   Each form of city government has certain advantages and disadvantages, depending on the criteria used for evaluation.

Separation of Powers   The strong-mayor and mayor-manager forms allow for separate legislative and executive branches. In the absence of a separation of powers, certain problems arise. With the council-manager form, voters probably consider the *policy* positions of city council candidates, unaware of the impact their votes might have on the selection of the manager.

Leadership   In most larger metropolitan areas, the more effective leadership made possible by the strong-mayor system is preferred. Although the council-manager

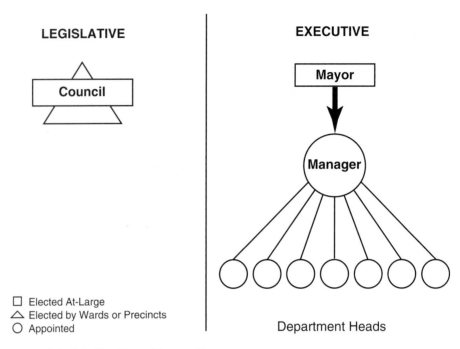

LEGISLATIVE

Council

☐ Elected At-Large
△ Elected by Wards or Precincts
○ Appointed

EXECUTIVE

Mayor

Manager

Department Heads

FIGURE 8.4 The Mayor-Manager Form

form may be more efficient, the manager cannot offer the kind of leadership possible under a strong-mayor structure. The strong mayor is not only the chief executive, but also wields the kind of community influence that comes from being an elected official. This is the sort of power respected by utility companies, contractors, city councils, and state or national governments. Furthermore, developing new policies to meet metropolitan challenges requires decisive and concerted leadership, without which city councils often respond slowly and haphazardly; program implementation may be uncoordinated and ineffectual.

Many urban problems require the cooperation of city agencies, the council, and the community at large. For example, planning city development involves the cooperative efforts of virtually all city agencies, together with federal and state agencies as well as such private groups as financial institutions, developers, landowners, and commercial businesses.

A highly visible leader with effective executive powers might be able to coordinate public and private sectors in the event of a disaster such as a riot or massive flood. New York's strong mayor was able to respond effectively to terrorist attacks on the World Trade Center. The immediate need was to secure the public's cooperation with police, fire, and civil defense departments. Subsequent reconstruction is being facilitated by an effective leader with political connections in state and national capitals. Efforts of city agencies must be coordinated with investors, developers, and other interested parties.

Although party lables do not appear on city ballots, Houston Mayor Bill White is a Democrat who worked successfully with a Republican majority on the city council. Personality goes a long way toward making nonpartisan leadership possible.

On the other hand, the charter is only one element of leadership. Effective leadership is certainly possible within other forms of city government when there is a crisis, or when strong personalities merge in a favorable political climate. Some strong mayors are incompetent leaders; others abuse the substantial powers of their office.

Responsibility   Perhaps it is the abuse of executive power that led many cities to adopt weak-mayor and commission charters that divide administrative duties among several directly elected officers. However, these arrangements do not guarantee responsible leadership. Voters are frequently confused and frustrated by the need to vote to fill poorly publicized minor offices. Corruption and inefficiency may, therefore, go unpunished at the polls.

Greater responsibility results when executive functions are more clearly defined and placed in the hands of a single executive who supervises the daily activities of administrative agencies. In the strong-mayor-council form, voters may hold a highly visible strong mayor accountable. Under the council-manager system the council may easily dismiss an irresponsible manager. Such clear and unified lines of executive responsibility make it possible both to give credit where it is due and to assess blame when necessary.

Efficiency and Responsiveness   Reputedly, the efficient forms of city government are those that rely on trained professional managers and utilize a merit system for hiring—the council-manager and mayor-manager types. The argument is that professional management results in better and more services for each dollar spent.

On the other hand, some raise the questions: Efficient at what? Which services are provided to whom, and under what circumstances?

Because professional managers are not elected politicians, council-manager governments operate in a less politicized environment than those forms in which chief executives are directly elected. Citizen interest and voter turnout are usually lower, especially among the poor and minority groups.

Because managers are not directly elected, they are open to the suspicion that they are not responsive to individual citizen complaints. Is the pothole in front of a driveway more likely to be filled by an elected executive seeking votes, or by a manager concerned with the most efficient use of the road crew?

On the other hand, the strong-mayor-council form tends to be more *political*. We sometimes view it as "mere politics" when public officials curry favor with other interest groups and individuals, but when they do us a favor or provide us a service, we see it is "responsive government." "Politics" and "responsive government" are two sides of the same coin—in theory, it is in forcing a politician to seek votes that democracy emerges.

Municipal Elections

City elections are administered by city officials and are held at times separate from general elections in order to help insulate cities from the influence of national, state, and county politics.

Nonpartisan Elections   Unlike general elections for state and county officials, Texas municipal elections are *nonpartisan,* as political parties do not officially participate in them. Because party primaries are not used to reduce the field of candidates, any qualified individual may file for a ballot position. Voters often must choose among numerous individuals without the party endorsements that may give them cues as to candidates' positions or political allegiances. Frequently, voters are confused, turnout is low, and elections are decided by a small group of activists.

By advocating nonpartisan elections, urban reformers hoped to reduce the influence of city machines and extraneous party issues. However, making municipal elections nonpartisan did not make them nonpolitical. In some communities, nonpartisan citizens' organizations dominated by higher-income individuals and business groups were able to substitute their influence for that of political parties. In most communities, city politics became more individualized and candidates became especially dependent on well-financed campaigns rather than on parties to get their message to the voters.

At-Large Elections   In most smaller cities, council candidates run citywide (at-large) rather than from neighborhood districts. The candidates receiving the most votes among the entire field of candidates are elected. In some cities, candidates file for specific council seats (the *place system*); rather than running against all candidates, they run only against those who have filed for that particular seat. Council members elected at-large are assumed to represent the entire city, and such arrangements probably work well enough in less populated, homogenous communities. In larger cities, however, citywide campaigns are expensive and ethnic or political minorities have little chance of being elected.

District Elections   Either voluntarily or because of voting-rights lawsuits, many larger communities now elect council members from single-member districts (wards). The council divides the city into equally populated areas and each neighborhood elects a single member to the council. Minorities, often concentrated in a few neighborhoods, are more likely to be elected. Voters may choose from fewer candidates and have an identifiable member to serve as their advocate and whom they can hold accountable.

Some cities elect a portion of the council in districts, and the remainder at-large. They hope members elected in districts will provide minority representation and a neighborhood perspective, while those elected at-large will represent the community as a whole.

SPECIAL DISTRICTS

Special districts are *limited-purpose* governments, each performing a narrow range of functions. They are more numerous and varied in origin, purpose, structure, and organization than *general-purpose* governments such as cities and counties.

Independent School Districts

Over 1,000 independent school districts serve as the basic structure for local control of the states' elementary and secondary schools. Voters in each independent school district elect seven or nine members (depending on the school district population) at-large or from single-member election districts for three- or four-year terms. These trustees set the district's tax rate, select textbooks from a state-approved list, and determine school policies within the guidelines established by the Texas Education Agency (TEA). They approve the budget for instructional supplies and construction, and the hiring and firing of personnel. Their most important decision is the hiring of a professional superintendent, whose policy recommendations the board usually accepts. The superintendent is also responsible for the executive or administrative functions of the school district.

At the state level, the TEA establishes standards for operating public schools and requires management, cost-accounting, and financial reports from local districts. It calculates the state funding available to local districts according to formulas for the foundation school program and provides money for textbook purchases.

The TEA is governed by the State Board of Education (SBE), whose members are elected to four-year overlapping terms from fifteen single-member districts. The SBE establishes general rules and guidelines for the TEA. The board approves organizational plans and recommends a budget to the governor and Legislative Budget Board.

The SBE recommends candidates for commissioner of education. This individual is appointed by the governor with the consent of the senate. The commissioner serves as the state's principal executive officer for education and is assigned a number of assistant and associate commissioners as well as a professional staff, who carry out the regulations and policies established by the legislature and the SBE concerning public-school programs. As professionals, the commissioner and staff have the necessary experience and training to make recommendations to the SBE and influence its decisions.

Other Special Districts

Purpose   In addition to independent school districts, there are also fifty community college districts. Non-school districts include metropolitan transit authorities, water districts, hospital districts, housing authorities, river authorities, municipal utility districts (MUDs), soil conservation and reclamation districts, flood-control districts, navigation districts, rural fire-prevention districts, airport authorities, and so on. Non-school districts have grown in number to 2,245, and extensive reliance on these districts is likely to continue.

Origins   State constitutional provisions authorize the legislature to create specific special districts such as the hospital districts in Comanche County and Hidalgo County. General constitutional provisions authorize the legislature to create airport authorities, rural fire-prevention districts, jail districts, and emergency-services districts. Some special districts, such as the Edwards Aquifer Authority, were created by a special legislative statute. Others, such as municipal utility districts (MUDs), are general-law districts, initiated by residents' petition with the approval of a majority of those voting in the proposed district.

There are several reasons for establishing special districts. Community college and independent school districts are established to offer a specialized service that is professionally managed and independent of the routine politics of general-purpose governments. Some are established because a need transcends existing political jurisdictions; for example, river authorities are useful because water flow does not respect the boundaries of counties or other governments. Community college districts provide higher education for residents of several independent school districts, and metropolitan transit authorities extend the public transportation system across several city boundaries. Some special districts have been created by the agreement of two or more existing local governments to eliminate duplication—such as metropolitan health districts, which have enabled some cities and counties to consolidate similar health services.

Certain special districts provide a needed service that general governments cannot or will not provide. Creating special districts can be easier than dealing with bureaucratic "turf wars" that might result from attempting to incorporate a new service into the existing structure of a city or county. General governments may avoid tax or bond limits by establishing a special district to provide a service they cannot otherwise afford; for example, hospital districts provide indigents with health services that would be too costly to finance using county tax revenues.

Land developers arrange the creation of districts such as MUDs to provide utilities and finance other improvements to their raw land. Land buyers in such developments are sometimes surprised to learn that they are paying taxes to retire bonds that the developers used to finance the basic infrastructure in their neighborhood.

Structure   Special districts are usually governed by multimember boards that make policy and appoint an executive director or manager to administer the day-to-day affairs of the district. In some districts these boards are elected by voters; in others they are appointed by existing general governments. Some special districts may tax property; others depend largely or entirely on grants from other governments; still others generate revenues from fees they charge for their services.

Evaluating Special Districts

Some special districts are effectively managed, fairly well publicized, and responsible. However, the large number and small size of special districts have created problems in many instances.

Critics argue that they are simply too small to be efficient. They are poorly funded and management can be amateurish. Purchasing in small quantities results in higher prices, and a small tax base results in higher interest payments if bonds are sold. Because of the size and limited purpose of special districts, the media and voters are often inattentive; most special districts are largely invisible to the average resident. The sheer number and variety of special districts can be baffling to voters. Creation of special districts may result in the election of more officials and the lengthening of the ballot. Governing boards are often elected separately from the general election, and voter turnout is low.

Of course, these problems could be overcome by consolidating smaller special districts into larger, more efficient, and highly visible ones. Some could be eliminated altogether and their functions assumed by general governments. Increased supervision by state, county, or city authorities might also improve efficiency and responsibility.

COGs

The proliferation of local governments has immensely complicated the process of planning and coordination. As a result, voluntary regional associations of local governments, called councils of governments (COGs), have been established in all areas of Texas. They offer regional planning and research services, operate training programs, and coordinate grant applications to the federal government. But while COGs are useful, they cannot completely eliminate duplication or impose rational planning in an otherwise uncoordinated system.

CONCLUSION

The number of local governments is large and growing because of the proliferation of special districts. The Texas legislature has created 254 county governments to provide state services and other functions at a geographically accessible level. Much of county governmental structure is established in the state constitution, and difficult to change. State statutes can affect their structure, but there is no provision for county home-rule charters. County commissioners make policy, but the executive function is decentralized in many elective and appointive offices. The result is a long ballot from which voters must choose from poorly publicized candidates.

Municipalities are more flexible than counties because smaller cities may choose their structure among several options allowed by statute. If their population exceeds 5,000, they may write their own charter.

The weak-mayor council form gives policymaking to the council, but executive power is decentralized among numerous elective and appointive officers. The strong-mayor council form allows the council to make policy and unifies lines of administrative responsibility in the mayor, who acts as a chief executive with appointive, removal, directive, and budgetary powers. In the council-manager form, the council makes policy and hires a professional manager to administer it. All Texas cities hold nonpartisan elections, and council members are elected at-large or in districts.

Special districts are numerous and extremely varied in origin, purpose, efficiency, structure, and power. They are often small, poorly publicized, and inefficient.

In general, local governments are geographically closer to the people and small enough for citizens to exercise greater control over them than state or national governments. Unfortunately, their politics generate little voter interest, and control is left to small numbers of people, political activists, and special interests.

KEY TERMS

ad valorem

annexation

at-large elections

city charter

council-manager form

extraterritorial
  jurisdiction

general-law city

home rule

incorporation

mayor-council form

mayor-manager form

special districts

strong-mayor form

wards

Logging On

The Texas Association of Counties provides links to news, issues, and laws relating to Texas counties. Go to **http://www.county.org/**.

The Texas Municipal League advocates city interests and publishes a variety of useful information about cities. Go to **http://www.tml.org/**.

Most major cities in Texas have their own Web sites representing different types of city government. See Mayor-Council *Houston* at **http://www. houstontx. gov/**. Read about the Houston city charter at **http:// www.lwvhouston.com/CityManual/chapter 2F.html**.

Council-Manager *Dallas* at **http://dallascityhall. com**. Read the Dallas city charter at **http://www. dallascityhall.com/dallas/eng/pdf/cao/01Chartr.pdf**.

San Antonio at **http://www.ci.sat.tx.us/**. Go to the city charter (at **http://www.sanantonio.gov/clerk/ charter/charter.htm**) and note the manner of selection and powers of city officials.

Austin at **http://www.ci.austin.tx.us/**. For other Texas municipalities, go to **http://www.tml.org/,** click on links and then on Texas cities.

For a look at education special districts, go to the Texas Education Agency at **http://www.tea.state.tx.us/**. For laws and rules governing special districts, see **http://www.capitol.state.tx.us/statutes/**.

Councils of Governments are regional planning organizations that try to coordinate the activities of local governments in their region. Go to **http:// www.txregionalcouncil.org/** and click on regional councils for the COG in your area.

ENDNOTE

1. U.S. Department of Commerce, Bureau of the Census, *2002 Census of Governments,* Vol. 1: *Government Organization* (Washington, D.C.: U.S. Government Printing Office, 2002).

Appendix

Public Policy: Issues, Problems, and Research

Texas, like all states, has assumed a major responsibility for administering and financing a wide variety of public services, but the vast majority of state spending is for public education, transportation, and welfare. Conflicting values and group interests in each of these areas of public policy is the essence of state politics.

TAX AND SPENDING POLICIES

According to either of the standard measures of the 2004 tax burden—per capita ($1,244) or as a percentage of personal income (4.8 percent)—Texas has among the lowest levels of state taxation in the nation. Demonstrate Texas's conservative culture for yourself by comparing the fifty state tax levels. The U.S. Bureau of Census tax data is conveniently reported in Legislative Budget Board, *Fiscal Size-Up 2004–05,* pp. 47–52.

Texas's general sales tax of 6.25 percent of the retail price of most items sold generates most (58 percent) of the state tax revenue, and there are a variety of selective sales or excise taxes on such specific items as alcohol, tobacco, and motor fuels. Severance taxes (on oil and natural gas production), and some business taxes account for a small share of state revenue. Examine Texas *tax* sources (Figure 1) and *Fiscal Size-Up 2004–05,* p. 24. Keep in mind that much state revenue is from other sources, especially the federal government (33 percent) and some earnings on state investments. Detailed data concerning tax collection is also available in reports published by the Comptroller of Public Accounts, *Annual Cash Report and Comprehensive Annual Financial Report* **(http://www.window. state.tx.us).**

Texas relies more than most states on various types of sales taxes and is one of only four states that has neither a personal nor a corporate income tax. Compare

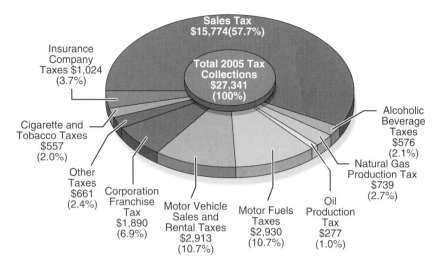

Sales Tax
$15,774(57.7%)

Total 2005 Tax
Collections
$27,341
(100%)

Insurance
Company
Taxes $1,024
(3.7%)

Cigarette and
Tobacco Taxes
$557
(2.0%)

Other
Taxes
$661
(2.4%)

Corporation
Franchise
Tax
$1,890
(6.9%)

Motor Vehicle
Sales and
Rental Taxes
$2,913
(10.7%)

Motor Fuels
Taxes
$2,930
(10.7%)

Oil
Production
Tax
$277
(1.0%)

Natural Gas
Production Tax
$739
(2.7%)

Alcoholic
Beverage
Taxes
$576
(2.1%)

F I G U R E 1 Texas Net Tax Collections by Source, Estimated for 2005 (in millions of dollars)

SOURCE: Legislative Budget Board, *Fiscal Size-Up 2004–05* (Austin: Legislative Budget Board, 2004), p. 24.

state financial data collected by the Bureau of Census and reported by the Council of State Governments, *The Book of the States 2005* (Lexington, Kentucky).

Texas sales and other consumer taxes are regressive because they fall more heavily on lower-income people who spend a larger percentage of their incomes to purchase the essentials of life. Local property taxes in Texas, among the highest in the nation, are also regressive. Liberal groups oppose such taxes because they unfairly fail to take into account a citizen's ability to pay, thereby reducing consumption that drives two-thirds of the American economy. The labor-supported Citizens for Tax Justice **(http://www.ctj.org/)** opposes regressive taxes. Click on various current tax issues presented by this organization.

In contrast, progressive tax rates, such as income taxes, increase as the tax basis increases and weigh more heavily on higher income persons with greater ability to pay. Supporters of progressive taxes argue that poor and middle-class families demand and spend most of their incomes for goods and services in ways that support the economy. Income taxes are the major source of revenue in only about fifteen states. Conservatives criticize progressive taxes because they view economic justice as allowing individuals to enjoy the maximum reward generated by their own personal efforts. Conservatives also argue for supply-side economics (that cutting taxes on high-income taxpayers and businesses creates a greater incentive for them to save and invest in the economy). Examine the conservative view effectively represented by the Texas Taxpayers and Research Association **(http://www.ttara.org/)**.

State spending patterns also reflect Texas's conservative political culture. Per capita state spending consistently ranks among the lowest of the fifty states—89 percent of the fifty-state average for education, 68 percent of average for public

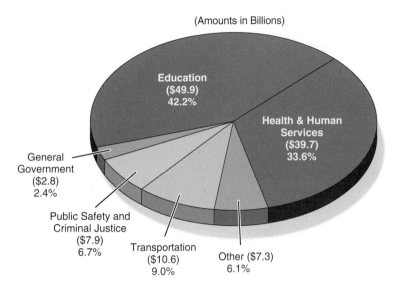

(Amounts in Billions)

Education
($49.9)
42.2%

Health & Human
Services
($39.7)
33.6%

General
Government
($2.8)
2.4%

Public Safety and
Criminal Justice
($7.9)
6.7%

Transportation
($10.6)
9.0%

Other ($7.3)
6.1%

TOTAL $118.2 Billion

FIGURE 2 State Appropriations by Function, 2004–2005 Biennium (in billions of dollars)

SOURCE: Legislative Budget Board, *Fiscal Size-Up, 2004–05* (Austin: Legislative Budget Board, 2004), pp. 12, 344.

welfare, and only 83 percent of average for highways. Figure 2 demonstrates that Texas spends more than four-fifths of the state budget for these three state services.

STATE SERVICES, POLICIES, AND ISSUES

Public Education

Public Education (K through 12) is a joint state-local responsibility. A fifteen-member elected State Board of Education nominates the commissioner of education, who is appointed by the governor. Together, the board and commissioner govern the Texas Education Agency, set state standards, and fund local school districts.

Seven- or nine-member elected boards govern more than a thousand local school districts according to standards set by the TEA and state law. Educational law and finance are described in *Educator's Guide to Texas School Law* published by the University of Texas Press. Public school finances are discussed at **http:// www.tea.state.tx.us/school.finance/**.

Conflicting group values are especially apparent as educational institutions establish curriculum and adopt textbooks. Compare the viewpoints presented at Mel Gabler's Christian conservative site **(http://www.textbookreviews.org/)** with the more secular views of the Texas Freedom Network **(http://www.tfn.org/)** and the People for the American Way **(http://www.pfaw.org/pfaw/general/)**.

Evaluate public school performance with a variety of statistical information provided by such sources as the National Center for Educational Statistics **(http://www.nces.ed.gov/edstats/)**. Since the National Commission on

Educational Excellence published *A Nation at Risk* in 1983, the allegation that public schools are failing has been used to drive numerous political agendas.

Some parent or teacher groups advocate devoting greater resources to public education. The American Federation of teachers reported that average Texas public school teacher salaries ($39,972, in 2002–2003) ranked thirtieth among the fifty states (13 percent below the national average). See **www.aft.org/salary** and other similar state-by-state comparisons. Conservative groups question if increased spending contributes to improved educational quality **(http://www.cato.org/pubs/pas/pa-298es.html).**

An increasingly common reform is to hold public schools accountable by implementing high-stakes student tests such as the Texas Assessment of Knowledge and Skills (TAKS) test. The American Educational Research Association **(http://www.aera.net/)** discusses such tests. See the American Association of School Administrators **(http://www.aasa.org)** and the American Federation of Teachers' state-by-state analysis of educational standards in *Making Standards Matter 2001* **(http://www.aft.org/edissues/standards/msm2001/).**

While charter and magnet schools offer greater choice in public schools, conservative and religious organizations are the most vocal advocates of vouchers to provide public funding to subsidize public school students to transfer to private schools. They argue that private and parochial school students learn more and that competition would be an incentive for public schools to improve—see Voucher Wars **(http://www.cato.org/).** Opponents such as the Anti-Defamation League fear such programs drain financial resources and the best students from public schools and risk excessive entanglement of government in religion (search for vouchers at **http://adl.org/**). To evaluate the success of voucher programs, see William G. Howell and Paul Peterson, *The Education Gap: Vouchers and Urban Schools* (Brookings Press, 2001).

Compare contrasting special-interest group views on a variety of education issues presented by the conservative National Center for Policy Analysis (search for education at **http://www.ncpa.org/**), and compare with the more liberal American Federation of Teachers **(http://www.aft.org/issues/)** and the National Education Association **(http://www.nea.org/issues/).**

Human Services and Welfare

The very definition of "welfare" is itself a politically charged controversy. Some use the term to refer to a broad range of government services or unearned benefits. Groups as diverse as Ralph Nader's liberal Public Citizen group and the conservative Cato Institute point to numerous examples of "corporate welfare" (see **http://www.corporations.org/welfare/**). Also consider government benefits such as small business subsidies and social security that substantially benefit the middle class. However, "welfare" is traditionally most often used to refer to programs to help the poor, based on a means test (making a low income the qualification for benefits).

Contrast differing views of the extent and causes of poverty. The Heritage Foundation reflects the conservative view that poverty rates are exaggerated

(Robert Rector, "The Myth of Widespread American Poverty" at **http://www. heritage.org/Research/Welfare/povinequal.cfm**); in contrast, see official definitions and poverty statistics at **http://aspe.hhs.gov/poverty/04poverty. shtml.**

Evaluate the proper role of state government in dealing with poverty. Approximately 3.4 million Texans (including 1.3 million children) live in families with incomes below the official poverty level (see **http://nccp.org/state_detail_ demographic_TX.html**). Texas's 15.6 percent poverty rate is one of the highest among the states (see Center for Public Policy Priorities, *Texas Poverty 101: Policy Brief* at **http://www.cppp.org/files/8/poverty101.pdf**). A large share of those in poverty benefit from the federal "food stamp" program, but only approximately 270,000 receive the state's Temporary Aid to Needy Families (TANF), monthly cash grants averaging $67 per child. Note limited eligibility requirements (**http://www. dhs.state.tx.us/programs/Texas Works/TANF.html**). When medical benefits (Medicaid), food stamps, and TANF grants are combined, recipients still fall 23 percent below the poverty level.

Transportation

Texas's financial commitment to its highway system has declined. The once-powerful Texas Good Roads and Transportation Association (**http://www. tgrta.com/**) is now less successful in promoting its agenda. Per-capita state spending for highways ranks forty-fourth among the states. Like most states, Texas spends little of its federal transportation grants for public mass transportation (**http://www.dot.state.tx.us/**). Evaluate the social and personal costs and benefits of dependence on personal motor vehicles instead of mass transportation.

Survey the other state services and spending programs in the Legislative Budget Board, *Fiscal Size Up 2004–05* (**http://www.lbb.state.tx.us/**). Note public policy trends and news in the fifty states at **http://www.stateline.org/ live/ViewPage.action.**

Index